Achieving Objectives Made Easy!

Practical

Goal Setting Tools

to enable you get what you want.

Proven

Time Management Techniques

for making the most of your valuable time.

Raymond Le Blanc

Published by Cranendonck Coaching, Maarheeze, The Netherlands.

ISBN 978-90-79397-03-7

Library of Congress Cataloging-in-Publication Data:
Le Blanc, Raymond Ph.
Achieving Objectives Made Easy! / Raymond Ph. Le Blanc
1. Time Management. 2. Goal Setting (Psychology) 3. Success

1.0

Dedication

This book is dedicated to the loving memory of my dad, F. J. Le Blanc. Thanks for reading to me. Thanks for listening to me. Thanks for being there. Always.

About the author

Raymond Le Blanc holds a master's degree in economics from the Erasmus University Rotterdam and a master's degree in clinical psychology from the Open University in Heerlen. He is also a NLP master practitioner.

After pursuing a career in banking, he switched emphasis to combine his passions. He now coaches people to discover and live fulfilling lives and writes nonfiction. He is the author of What You Should Know about Autism Spectrum Disorders and Singapore: The Socio-Economic Development of a City-State. He lives with his wife Karin and their two children, Brigitte and Vincent, in the village of Maarheeze, the Netherlands.

About the book

Discover Raymond Le Blanc's powerful time management methods and goal setting techniques to turn around every area of your life—at home or at work.

Engaging and down-to-earth, author Le Blanc walks you step by step through practical goal setting techniques to enable you to reach previously unreachable dreams and goals, while his proven time management methods teach you innovative ways to make the most of your valuable time.

With *Achieving Objectives Made Easy* you will

- Develop a mission and a vision for your career and personal life
- Learn strategies for setting and achieving goals
- Implement habits key to success
- Beat procrastination
- Gain motivation
- Take control of your time
- Watch your dreams become reality

All in twenty minutes a day.

Author Raymond Le Blanc has helped numerous people with his easy-to-understand self-management techniques.

Contents

Preface...7

Introduction...8

PART ONE: What Do You Want?...9

Go Ahead—Dream...10

Your Current State of Affairs...14

Your Personal Values...20

PART TWO: Goal Setting..22

Your Mission..23

Your Vision...26

Goal Setting: Who..28

Goal Setting: What..30

Goal Setting: Why...31

Goal Setting: How...33

Goal Setting: When...37

Write Your Goals...38

Create an Action Plan...40

Why People Fail to Set and Achieve Goals..........................42

Habits that Bring Success..52

Character Matters...54

Goal Setting: Final Insights...56

PART THREE: Time Management..60

What Is Time Management?...61

Your Current State of Affairs...64

Activity Logs..67

The Monetary Value of Your Time......................................70

Use Your Personal Prime Time...73

Eliminate Your Energy Drainers...75

Focus on Your Strengths...79

How Your Personality Comes into Play...............................81

Beat Procrastination..83

The Power of Motivation...86

Communication...91

Delegate..95

Scheduling...99

Organize Your Work Space...101

Streamline Your Tasks...105

Snuff Out Time Robbers..107

The Ultimate Time Management Tool...116

Time-Saving Devices..126

Routines...128

Commit to Life's Goals...132

How to Get in Contact... 134

Bibliography...135

Preface

After finishing university and accepting my first job, I married, made a career, raised children . . . you get the idea. Always too many things to do and too little time to do them. Eventually I noticed this wasn't making me happy.

Then I was appointed managing director at a bank where I was responsible for the day-to-day running of the company, and for developing business plans for the long-term future of the organization. We had several major problems that had to be tackled almost simultaneously. We prepared for the introduction of the Euro, the coming of the new millennium, the building of a new headquarters, and a change in focus. Two projects (Euro and Millennium) were unprecedented. I was under tremendous pressure.

To get through it, I studied time management, goal setting, and self-management. I soon found I had more time for myself and my family despite the high demands of my job. I achieved more in less time, and my level of stress declined.

I enthusiastically applied this knowledge to other areas of my life, and decided to take my career down a new path. I received my master's degree in psychology, and made the transition from banker to clinical psychologist.

As a psychologist and NLP coach, I've helped many people cope with similar problems: overwhelm, exhaustion, even defeat. I developed a new approach that blends existing ideas with my experience. The valuable techniques I use in this approach are provided in this book. They are the foremost (and easiest!) methods to enable you to make more time for yourself and to achieve your desired goals.

I would like to thank Tammy Barley for helping me finish this book. Her ideas and suggestions were very valuable.

Introduction

We heap our daily schedules full of activities. Despite time-saving conveniences like cell phones, computers and the Internet, we rarely have enough time for our work, our families, friends, or ourselves. So many activities daily demand our attention that it can be difficult to make plans, even if those plans would ease our burdens down the road.

We are busy, but are we productive with our time?

Many people fail to achieve what they want and what they dream of simply because they haven't yet discovered the secrets of goal setting and time management.

Managing your time and setting goals are interwoven topics. A healthy time-management plan encompasses goal setting. Achieving goals is only possible when the time factor is considered. With the aid of this book, you can learn to excel at both, free up your time, and accomplish more than you thought possible.

Whether you're a newbie to goal setting and time management or you've delved into similar books on the subject before, this book has a lot to offer you. It goes beyond presenting techniques; it teaches you, step by step, page by page, how to achieve what you've only dared to dream of before. That dream is now in reach.

It's time to go get it.

Throughout this book you will be asked to answer questions that will help you on your way. It would be handy to grab a notebook or a journal (we'll call it a journal, for simplicity's sake) and a pen or pencil, and keep them within arm's reach.

To make the most effective use of this book, I recommend you read and put into practice just one simple step—only twenty minutes or so—a day, to begin relieving your stress, reaching for success, and perhaps even discover something unexpected about yourself.

It's all in here.

Let the journey begin.

PART ONE: What Do *You* Want?

Chapter One

Go Ahead—*Dream*

This book is about far more than how to set goals and manage your time. It's about how to use proven goal-setting and time-management techniques to help you succeed and to achieve what you've only dared to dream of.

So let's cut right to it. What do you want? What will bring you happiness?

Since the fourth or fifth grade, we've been conditioned to see ourselves as having "limits." Children are born free of mental baggage. They see themselves as capable of doing and being anything they choose. That's why kids dream of being astronauts or explorers or movie stars. But as we get older our minds get shackled. We slowly give up our dreams to fear, worry, or feelings of lacking. Because of negative feelings and fears, few of us attempt such big dreams. Instead, we settle for the ordinary and as a result fall into a "reality" trap.

Vow to stop putting down your dreams!

Here are some big dreams that people often put off:

- Visiting that country
- Writing that book
- Having that baby
- Attending that seminar
- Getting that degree
- Learning that language
- Starting that Internet business

What do you truly want? Take a few minutes. Think about it. This is the first—and a key—step toward achieving your goals. Let those long-awaited wants bubble to the surface. Keep in mind that this kind of dreaming is best done when you are feeling inspired and energized. Boundless.

Because the difference between living a fulfilling life and just living an average life is the quality of the goals you set for yourself.

So go ahead and dream.

🖊   The following list will help you to brainstorm.

If your life could be anything you wanted it to be, what would it be right now?
Where would you live? _____
What would your house be like? _____
Who would your friends be? _____
How would you spend your time if you could do anything you wanted? _____

What would you eat? Wear? Listen to? _____
Would you work? If so, what would you do? If not, what would you do? _____

What would you want to learn? To know? To be? _____
Where would you like to vacation? What would you do? _____
What else would be a part of your perfect life? List it all! _____

Are there things you really want and could easily have with the resources you have now,
but that you just haven't given yourself permission for?
What's the goal? _____
Why don't you have it? _____
What's the goal? _____
Why don't you have it? _____
What's the goal? _____
Why don't you have it? _____
Is there a pattern? If so, describe it: _____

Are there things that exist in your life right now that you'd be better off without? Habits, clutter, distressing people, unpleasant environmental factors, unnecessary expenses, fixations, collections, annoying verbal habits... Anything at all that you'd be better off without.
I want to eliminate _____
I want to eliminate _____

🖊   In your journal, write down whichever of your dreams you find important enough to want to achieve. (Goals   must be in writing. An unwritten want is just a wish. If it's in writing, it's real, big, and the beginnings of a commitment. Writing down your goal also makes the goal more powerful. It has been proven that when people write things down, they are more likely to focus on them and achieve their goals.)

Keep your list of dreams close. We'll use it again in the next chapter.

Chapter Two

Your Current State of Affairs

You have dreamed of what you want and written down a few solid goals. Excellent. Now here's a question. Once you reach those goals, will you enjoy satisfaction in all areas of your life?

Probably not all areas. Living a balanced life is important because we can be more content, more alive, and better enjoy each day. Living a balanced life means keeping balance in physical and spiritual aspects. So let's look at your current state of affairs to determine which other goals you may wish to set in order to bring that balance and happiness.

Here is a good way to help you measure your success (happiness) in several fields:

✐ Read the paragraphs below. Rate yourself on a scale of 1 to 100 (1 is low, 100 is high), asking yourself *how satisfied you are* with your finances and career, family and home, community and charity (your social side), spirituality and ethics, physical well-being and health, and mental and educational levels. Consider your answers carefully.

Finances and Career. Feeling happy with your career or business is an important ingredient to obtaining happiness in other aspects of your life. Having a stable financial situation provides a reserve essential to feeling good about who you are. Are you happy with your career, job, or business, or are you suffering in this area? Have you achieved a satisfactory standard of living? Have you created a stable financial situation where your personal assets grow monthly? Have you planned for your children's education? What about your own retirement?

My score _____

Family and Home. Family relationships give us a sense of belonging and insulate us from the challenges of the world. The love of one's spouse is a precious gift that continually needs to be worked on to grow. Raising a family can be a rich and rewarding experience and challenge. Establishing and preserving strong, productive family relations nurtures our self-esteem. Do you have close, loving, family relationships? Have you realized your dream in terms of your home and family relationships? Be sure to use your own personal standards rather than society's standards. Have you forgiven anyone who has hurt you, and have they forgiven you? Do you thank each other for the things that you do well, or do you sabotage each other?

My score _____

Community and Charity. We all are a part of a community. Having strong, flourishing relationships and the skills to get along well with others is crucial in order to experience strong self-esteem. We crave to belong, we need to belong. Do you make friends easily, and are they people who help build your self-esteem, or are they people who drain your self-esteem? Is there at least one other person with whom you can discuss important experiences? Do you have many rewarding, close, and loving relationships? Do you have interests outside your career and family (for example, sports, theater, outdoor events)? Are you happy with your contributions to charities and to the community you belong to?

My score _____

Spiritual Health. The spiritual dimension is your center, your commitment to your value system. Good spiritual health inspires and uplifts you. Do you take time regularly to read uplifting books or listen to personal development audios? Do you have your own clearly defined, written vision for what your life will be like, or do you merely go along with someone else's vision for your life? Are you in touch with your values, with your abilities, and with your life purpose? Are you living up to those personal values? Is religion important to you? If so, are you happy with the way you are practicing your religion?

My score _____

Physical Health. Positive, vibrant confidence comes from taking the best possible care of our health. The physical dimension involves caring for your physical body—eating the right foods, getting enough rest and relaxation, and exercising regularly. If we don't have a regular exercise program, eventually we will develop health problems. A good program builds your body's endurance, flexibility and strength. A new program should be started gradually, in harmony with the latest research findings. How satisfied are you with your current level of physical health? Do you exercise regularly? Are you fit enough to do everything you want to do? Is your diet leading to ideal health, or do you regularly eat junk food?

My score _____

Mental Health. It's important keep your mind sharp by reading, writing, organizing and planning. Read broadly and expose yourself to great minds. Did you carry out the educational goals you set for yourself following high school graduation? Are you still growing and learning? Do you regularly invest in your continuing education? Do you take the time to do the hobbies and activities that you love to do?

My score _____

Emotional Health. Emotional well-being is about how we feel, think and behave. Nobody feels blissfully happy, thinks positive thoughts and behaves sensibly all the time, but if you're in a good state of mind, it's much easier to enjoy life. Are you content with the way you treat, respond to, and interact with others? When you're alone, are you content with the way you think of others and of yourself?

My score _____

Individuality. Individuals tend to change their world in order to reach a desired state. Individuality is about being able to freely enjoy your own interests and point of view. Are you happy with your individual space? Do you feel there is room beyond your personal space for your individuality? Do you feel liberated? Do you feel free to choose the outlook or lifestyle you desire? Do you feel you are free to stand by your own convictions?

My score _____

Next, record your answers on the circular chart below by putting a dot on the spoke of each respective category. Assign the innermost notch on the wheel a value of 0, and the outer ring a value of 100. After you have marked all the spokes, connect your dots, creating your own wheel.

For example, it may look something like the example figure on the opposite page:

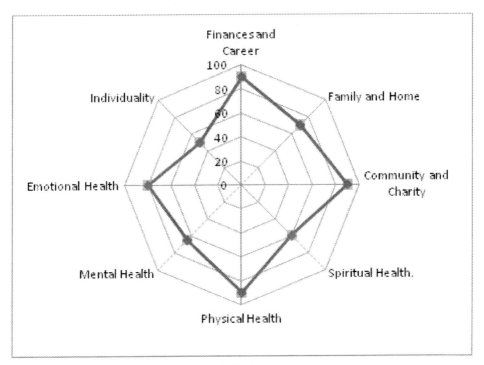

Figure 1: Example current state of affairs

This figure shows you a visual representation of a current state of affairs.

You can color the inside of the area marked by the thick line with a solid color if you prefer.

Figure 2: Another Example with colored area.

(This figure is inspired by the Wheel of life (Bhavacakra), an instructional figure in Buddhism.)

Now it's your turn.

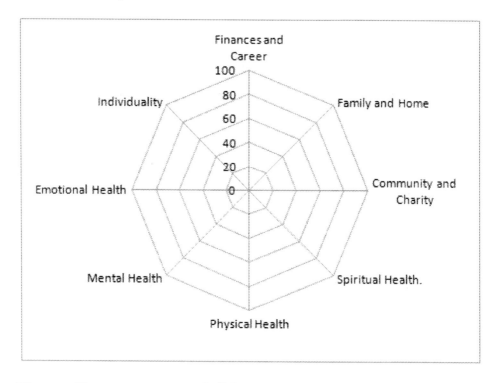

Figure 3: Your current state of affairs

The outcome of your current state of affairs shows your degree of satisfaction with several aspects of your life. The more solid color there is, the more balance you have, and the happier you are. If your circle is lopsided, the low score(s) reveal area(s) on which you might want to focus your goal-setting efforts. If your wheel is round but small, you may wish to set goals in all areas to expand your wheel and therefore your overall happiness.

Where might you benefit from making changes? Consider your low spots, the areas you are least satisfied with.

✎   To the list of dreams you made in your journal, add the areas you want to improve upon (*I want to improve upon:*).

Next, rewrite that list—one item per page—in their order of importance to you. As you will soon see, this will help you to effectively and quickly reach those objectives.

Congratulations! You now have the beginnings of a few or several goals you would like to achieve.

The wheel can serve as a focal point from which you measure your change. I recommend you take a look at your state of affairs monthly. You can use the information your wheel provides to see in which areas you are showing improvement and where you may want to put in some extra work.

Up until now we've focused on things you want. Next let's focus on *you*.

Chapter Three

Your Personal Values

Values are traits or qualities that are considered worthwhile; they represent an individual's highest priorities and deeply held driving forces. A value is that for which you make a stand.

What do values have to do with goal setting?

Simply this. If the goals you set are out of alignment with your values, it will make those goals extremely difficult to achieve. For instance, if you value integrity, it probably wouldn't be wise to want to become the most successful hard-selling door-to-door salesperson of useless products.

The step of defining your values is important; effective people identify and develop a clear, concise and understood meaning of their values. Once defined, values impact every aspect of your choices, work behavior, interpersonal interaction, contributions, and the goals you set.

You might hold different values for work and for your private life. But as the lines between your professional and personal lives become less defined, it's important that you create symmetry and provide balance between both so that, as much as circumstances allow, you can be yourself. If you can't be you, how can you be happy?

Following are some examples of values. You might use these as the starting point for introspection into your own values.

I value:

- accountability
- accuracy
- ambition
- authenticity
- compassion
- competency
- courage
- creativity

- credibility
- dedication
- dependability
- dignity
- discipline
- efficiency
- empathy
- flexibility
- friendliness
- generosity
- honesty
- humility
- independence
- innovativeness
- integrity
- loyalty
- persistency
- respectfulness
- responsibility
- truthfulness

In your journal, on a fresh page, list of your personal values (*My Personal Values*). If you have difficulty determining them, ask yourself, "What's most important to me in life?" until you run out of answers.

Next, see if you can group them according to common themes—you will likely discover a mere handful of values govern your existence.

Lastly, sort them by the importance you give them. To find out which values are most important to you, establish a hierarchy by asking yourself, "What's more important for me to feel: _____ or _____?"

Great. You made stock of the values that are important to you and tried to find clusters of values that pop up often. Look over your values and their hierarchy once more. If, for example, dependability, friendliness, and loyalty tops your list, that may suggest working with others is of higher value to you than working alone.

Flag the page that lists your personal values. With the insight the list provides, you can be sure to set goals in alignment with those values. That will make your goals easier to achieve.

Now you know what you want. You know what will bring you happiness. So let's go get it.

PART TWO: Goal Setting

Chapter Four

Your Mission

You have listed in order of importance your dreams and other plans you wish to achieve for your personal, and perhaps professional, success and happiness, and you know your values will be an important part of those plans.

So how do you make those plans happen?

It all begins with a mission statement.

Here's a dictionary definition of *mission*: "Purpose, reason for being; an inner calling to perform an activity or a service."

A mission statement is a brief and focused statement of purpose of the direction you want your goals to take you. Using a roadmap as an analogy, the mission statement is the highway you choose to take to get you from where you are to where you want to be, and includes the values with which you make your journey. Goals are the mile markers along the road to your destination. The goals and decisions you make both now and in the future should be based upon your mission statement.

When the mission statement is known, understood, accepted and communicated, positive things happen, and energy and effort are no longer wasted. With it, you will always know whether you are headed in the right direction.

Your personal mission statement will be unlike anyone else's. It will be customized to your unique talents and abilities.

There are three important properties your mission statement must have:

1. Unique—It must be yours and not anybody else's

2. Stimulating—It must stir you into action
3. Motivating—It must personally inspire you

Here's the basic structure of a mission statement:
To use my...(skills, talents)
to...(action)
so that...(result).

A mission statement should be no more than one sentence—usually twenty-five words or less—should be easily understood, and be able to be recited by memory. If you can write one that is short, clear, and resonates with your personal values, then you will have an inspiring mission statement.

Here are some examples. Notice the underlying values, not necessarily spelled out, in these mission statements:

- A mother's mission statement might read: *To use my talents* as a mother *to* coach my children through the early years of their lives *so that* they can look back on happy, carefree childhoods.
- A writer's statement might read: *To use my talents* as a writer *to* write moralistic plays that are entertaining or artistically pleasing *so that* I'll reach a large audience with my message.
- To create beautiful paintings so that others are inspired by and can enjoy them (an artist).
- Our mission is to offer a wide range of home furnishing items of good design and function, excellent quality and durability, at prices so low that the majority of people can afford to buy them (IKEA of Sweden).
- To use my knowledge and experience as a therapist to aid the regional depression support group so that people with a depression can be helped (a volunteer).
- To create magnificent buildings for social gatherings so that people can celebrate in maximum comfort (an architect).
- To support others in their work so that the team gets the best results (a manager).
- To organize the world's information and make it universally accessible and useful (Google).
- I use my talents and skills as a communicator to publish books and audio with the aim to help people live healthy and happy lives.

🖉 In your journal, on a fresh page, write your mission statement. Decide what it is you want, and make it clear and specific. This is precisely the purpose of your mission statement. Let this be a labor of love! Pour your heart, mind and soul into it, and if this is your first attempt at writing a mission statement, don't agonize over it. Just get something down. If it doesn't feel right, you can easily change it until it does or come back to it later.

It's useful to review your mission statement every three months. You can add to or alter your mission statement as needed. Place a copy of your mission statement where you can see it daily. It is there to motivate you.

Chapter Five

Your Vision

You've determined and ordered your dreams and other plans you wish to achieve, and the values with which you will achieve them, and you've written your mission statement, the roadmap that will keep you steady on the right course. You are four important steps closer to getting what you want.

The next step to setting and achieving your goals is your vision statement.

Here's a dictionary definition of *vision*: "A mental picture of the future we seek to create."

A vision statement describes the detailed mental picture of where you want to see yourself in the future once the mission has been carried out. It may describe how you see events unfolding over ten or twenty years if everything goes exactly as hoped and, like the mission statement, it includes your values.

Your vision is to be a reflection of your true core desires. It requires imagination and a positive "prophecy." Laurie Beth Jones, a best-selling author of several books including Creating Your Mission Statement for Work and Life, and The Four Elements of Success, encourages that, "One of the most important things we can do for others—and for ourselves—is to create and keep an atmosphere charged with positive prophecies." That is what vision statements do: they project into the future and create a desirable picture that motivates and inspires.

An effective vision statement:
1. Describes a bright future (hope)

2. Describes achievable ambitions
3. May include a date or age specification
4. Is memorable and engaging

What is the difference between a mission and vision statement? If the mission statement is your roadmap, the vision statement is your destination. It's the mental picture of where your mission will bring you.

For example, "We help transport goods and people efficiently and cost-effectively without damaging the environment" is a mission statement. "We will be one among the top three transporters of goods and people in North America by 2010" is a vision statement. It is concrete and unambiguous.

These are some other sample vision statements. Again, notice the underlying values:

- When I celebrate my sixtieth birthday, I notice many close friends and family enjoying our hospitality. When I enter my study overlooking our beautiful garden, there's a bookshelf filled with several books and CDs with my name on them as author. I feel happy and fulfilled.
- Within the next ten years, I see myself as the top sales agent in my region with a passion for service.
- Riverside is a safe community with pride, opportunity, friendliness and high quality of life for all generations. This is obvious by our cultural activities, quality schools, health care, recreation, jobs and people who have respect for each other and the community.
- My vision is that each customer to our shop finds the information or material he wants, when he wants it, in the format most fitting for his use.

✎ Ready to craft your vision statement? Take the time to build a clear image of the life you want (your vision), then write it in your journal, on a fresh page. Remember to include your values, or your vision won't be an accurate reflection of you.

When you have completed your vision, hold that image—focus on it daily. You may opt to rewrite it again and again, and if you do, mix it up a little. Picture yourself in different scenarios enjoying this result. You can add to or alter your vision statement as needed. Place a copy of your vision statement where you can see it daily. Like your mission statement, it is there to inspire you.

Chapter Six

Goal Setting: Who

In your journal you've listed dreams and things about yourself or your life you wish to improve, one item per page, in order of their importance to you. You've penned your mission statement—the roadmap you've chosen to follow—and your vision statement—your end result (how you view your future success and happiness).

In chapters 6 through 10, we will explore five components to consider whenever setting a goal: Who, What, Why, How, and When.

First, "Who."

Who is the person setting the goal? You, of course. But in which role?

When you take a close look at yourself and take note of your actions and thoughts during a day, you probably think of yourself as a pretty good actor, an actor who acts according to a script, and an actor with enormous improvising qualities matching the different demands that meet him/her all the time. This actor in us can manage a vast amount of roles.

All through life, you play different roles depending on what you are doing and to whom you are relating. For example, when you are talking with your parents your role is son or daughter, but when you are talking to your children your role is father or mother. At work you may at various times be a manager, a subordinate, a coworker. At other times you may be a trusted friend, a volunteer and so on.

Classifying your role is one of the five components that enables you to set a clear goal. Here are examples of different roles:

- father
- mother
- husband
- wife
- son
- daughter

- brother
- sister
- grandfather
- grandmother
- boyfriend
- girlfriend
- income provider
- volunteer
- boss
- employee
- project leader
- team member
- mentor
- student
- sportsman/ woman
- friend
- neighbor
- salesman
- writer

Which role will you play to achieve each of your goals?

✎ In your journal, on each page you wrote a dream or aspect of yourself you wish to set a goal to achieve, write: "Who" followed by the role you will play as you achieve that goal.

Chapter Seven

Goal Setting: What

The second component to consider whenever setting a goal is "What."

Simply put, "What" *is* your goal, written in the framework of a performance rather than an outcome.

This is very important. Goals written in the framework of outcomes are vulnerable to failure because of events that can happen beyond your control, such as bad business environments, poor judging, bad weather, injury, or just plain bad luck. There is nothing as dispiriting as failing to achieve a goal for reasons beyond your control.

If, on the other hand, you write your goals in the framework of personal performance or skills or knowledge to be acquired, then you will have greater control over achieving your goals and draw satisfaction from your accomplishment.

For example, you might achieve a personal best time in a race, but still be disqualified because of a poor judging decision. If you had set an outcome goal of being in the top three, then this will be a defeat. If, however, you set a performance goal of achieving a particular time, then you will have achieved the goal and can draw satisfaction and self-confidence from your accomplishment.

✎   In your journal, beneath each "Who," write: "What." Then rewrite the dream or aspect of yourself you wish to set a goal to achieve, in the framework of a performance.

Chapter Eight

Goal Setting: Why

The third component to consider whenever setting a goal is "Why."

Why do you want to achieve an objective? Most likely the answer is because you believe in or value that objective.

Finding your "Why" means finding your purpose, what drives you, what you are truly passionate about. Many people fail to achieve success simply because they lack clear reasons for doing so.

Incorporating the "Why" into your goals will enable you to achieve them while enjoying the steps you will take along the way.

Even the drudgery we sometimes have to deal with is easier to manage if we know why we must do it. Knowing "Why" will make necessary tasks a part of your plan, and thus a choice rather than a load.

The more compelling your reasons are, the greater your chances will be for accomplishing your goals. Conversely, if you can't come up with "good" reasons, you might as well move on to another objective, as this one won't be achieved.

Do you want $5 million at retirement? Why? You say you want to live in a mansion? Why?

There are no wrong answers here. "Whys" are the principles, standards, or qualities considered worthwhile or desirable by the person (or couple or family or team) who holds them. What one person or group thinks is vain or stupid, another will think is worthy or great. You must come up with reasons that are honest, strong, and motivating to you or your group. And the more "Whys" you have for each objective, the better.

Here is an example of "Why":

I want to reach my goal (become senior account manager) *because* I believe it is important for me to stay financially secure. And I value a career and feel responsible for maintaining a good income for my family.

You can also view "Whys," simply, as the list of benefits to you for reaching this goal.

For example, benefits for a fitness goal might include (again, this is a list) feeling great, clothes fit well and look good, and people compliment me.

If you have strong enough "Whys" for your goals, you are going to pursue your goals until you achieve them. Not achieving them would give you more pain than doing what needs to be done in order to realize your goals.

✎   Give serious thought why you want to achieve each of your objectives. In your journal, beneath each "What," write: "Why" followed by your reasons for wanting to achieve that objective, or simply write a list of benefits.

Review your "Whys" monthly, making adjustments when necessary, and you will find yourself becoming more motivated to strive toward your goals.

Chapter Nine

Goal Setting: How

The fourth component to consider whenever setting a goal is "How." "How" are you going to achieve your objective? To be able to do so, you must have the necessary *strategy* and *resources* in place.

Strategy

As a simple definition, "strategy" is the specific steps it will take to reach your goal.

For example, let's say your goal is this: "I want to go back to school and get a bachelor's degree in English by December 31st of next year." That's a decent goal, but you aren't just going to walk onto a college campus and be awarded a degree in English. You must determine which school to attend, how to pay for school, and how many classes to take at one time, among other details. There must be a strategy.

Let's take strategy even further, again considering the college goal.

Earning the degree itself is a pretty big goal. "How" are you going to achieve your objective? You can break it down into smaller goals. For instance, one of those smaller goals could be: "I want to finish four classes by the end of this year."

A goal may be short term, medium term or long term. Some people call everything under a week "short term," under six months "medium term," and over six months "long term." Others might choose different time frames.

Short-term goals are ones that you will achieve in the near future, such as within a day, within a week, or possibly within a few months. They are often the stepping-stones that lead up to medium- and long-term goals, and are a great way to progress through your plan. Those stepping-stones are your strategy. Short-term goals keep you from becoming overwhelmed or losing sight of your long-term goal. They give you steps to look forward to so that you can celebrate along the way to the larger goal.

What you decide you want to accomplish by next week, and where you decide you want to be in one year, or five, or even twenty, will have an impact on what you do today. Be ready to plan your strategy.

✐ Consider the goals you've written in your journal. Write "short-term" next to each short-term objective, "medium-term" next to each medium-term objective, and "long-term" next to each long-term objective. By doing so, you are beginning to plan your strategy, or the steps (short-term goals) you will take to reach those goals, to get you from here to there. Go ahead. I'll wait until you're done.

Welcome back. Next, for each medium- and long-term objective, list short-term objectives (and the "Who," "What," and "Why") needed to achieve the new short-term objectives.

For instance—using our roadmap analogy and an imagined scenario to go with it—let's say you want to drive from San Francisco to San Diego (that's your long-term goal). Your "Who" is "nephew," because you're driving to San Diego to see your uncle. Your "What" of course, is to arrive in San Diego. Your "Why" is because he adores you and he just won the lottery. Now, for such a long drive, it helps to make stops (short-term goals) along the way. Your first goal can be to get to San Jose. Your next goal will be to get to the 5 Freeway. And so on.

As best you can, write your own (real) short-term goals. (Hint: Write each new short-term goal on its own clean sheet of paper.) Go ahead. Yep, I'll wait.

Finished? Excellent. Next, for each medium- or long-term goal, arrange the new short-term goal, one behind the other, in the order they need to be accomplished in order to achieve the bigger objective. These new short-term goals will be your strategy.

Attach (clip, do not staple) these new pages to the original medium- or long-term objective page in your journal.

Resources

The other important aspect of determining "How" a goal will be carried out is the resources you have available, or will have available, to achieve that goal.

Resources are required to carry out a task. They can be people, equipment, facilities, funding, or anything else capable of or required for completing a goal.

An assistant is a resource, more education is a resource, and an encouraging mate is a resource. Other resources may include books, tapes, seminars you would like to attend, courses you would like to complete, mentors, and coaches.

A list of your resources is a valuable tool for making and accomplishing goals because you can instantly draw on resources to help you. If you don't currently have a certain, necessary resource available to you, you will need to determine when you will get it and how it will be obtained.

"How" are you going to achieve your objective using resources?

What is it you want to accomplish? If you want to start your own business in the next couple of years, then you know you have to set back cash (resource) to obtain this goal. You will also need to decide if you need extra skills (resource) or education (resource) to set up the business. Here you'll notice that resources and strategy go hand-in-hand. Resources are those people or items capable of or required for completing a goal. The actual planning of what you'll need and determining the steps you'll take to achieve them is strategy.

In an earlier example I planned to become a senior account manager. So I will volunteer to perform chores (strategy) with a friend of mine who is a senior account manager at another company, and while performing those chores, I'll ask him for some useful tips (resources).

The most important resource you have is . . . Guess who? . . . Yourself.

You might like to do what marketing consultants call a SWOT on yourself—this is where you analyze your Strengths, Weaknesses, Opportunities and Threats.

You'll probably only want to put your strengths and opportunities in your resources list. Think about your abilities—physically, mentally, and in terms of confidence. Your strengths and achievements in these areas are good resources for you to draw on. (We'll talk about this in more detail in chapter 23, "Focus on Your Strengths." Have a quick look if you'd like help with a few ideas.)

🖉 In your journal, beneath each "Why," write: "How: Resources Currently Available." List every resource you currently have available to you in terms of your own experience and outside resources. I'll wait.

Now, beneath each "How: Resources Currently Available," write: "How: Resources I Will Need to Obtain." List every resource you can think of that you currently do not have available but will need to obtain. Leave space to add to this list as additional thoughts or ideas for resources surface. I'll wait again.

Next, for each "How: Resources I Will Need to Obtain," write new short-term objectives—and the "Who," "What," and "Why"—needed to obtain that resource, each on a separate, clean sheet of paper. (You're likely getting the hang of this by now.)

Arrange the new short-term objectives in the order they need to be accomplished to achieve their resource objectives.

Attach (clip, do not staple) these new pages to the original medium- or long-term objective page in your journal, arranging them with other short-term goals, in the order they need to be accomplished.

As additional thoughts or ideas for resources surface, make and arrange new objectives—and the "Who," "What," and "Why"—needed to obtain their resource objectives.

Feel free to toss out each short-term objective page once you achieve its objective.

Review and adjust the resources you need to obtain and the strategy needed to carry out the "How" weekly.

Chapter Ten

Goal Setting: When

The fifth and final component to consider whenever setting a goal is "When."

All goals must have deadlines because it's a psychological law that work always expands to fill the time allowed. So goals we set must have target dates, time frames for completion.

For example, many of us may want to find a new job or start our own business. We spend a lot of time talking about what we want to do, someday. But without an end date there is no sense of urgency, no reason to take any action today. Having a specific time frame, a "When," gives you the impetus to get started. It also helps you check your progress.

✎   In your journal, beneath each "How," write: "When" followed by the date you want to accomplish that objective. (If you're getting quite a stack, now is a good time to select the one or two goals you most want to achieve, and set the others aside until you feel confident you can take on another goal.)

Chapter Eleven

Write Your Goals

In chapters 6 through 10, we explored the five components to consider whenever setting a goal: Who, What, Why, How, and When. In this chapter we will finally use that information to set actual goals.

Goal Cards

The goal card is a simple and incredibly powerful tool for writing and reaching your goals.

As you've learned, it's important to have goals . . . big and small, short-term and long-term, to enable you to achieve what you want. You've also learned that to effectively and quickly reach the goals that are most important to you, you must prioritize them on your list.

You need a way to stay centered on your most important goal(s), to get that goal burned into your subconscious mind. You can achieve this by having your goal(s) permanently available at arm's reach. A goal card is a great way to do that.

Using card stock, like an index card:
1. Write your deadline (the "When") at the top.
   For example: By August 15th of next year (or whenever your deadline is)
   (Note: This is the only part of your goal card that is written in future tense, and it's only for urgency. It's not part of your goal statement.)
2. Begin your goal statement by writing it in personal tense ("I")
3. Continue writing your goal in present tense ("I AM")

4. Write your goal with positive language and emotion ("I AM so happy")
5. Write your goal with gratitude ("I AM so happy and thankful")
6. Give added emphasis to personal and present tense ("I AM so happy and thankful now that I AM . . .")
7. Finish by filling in your goal, keeping the "Who," "What," "Why," and "How," and your personal values list and mission and vision statements in mind.

For the "What," remember that the goal MUST be stated in the positive. In other words, you must write what you want to achieve, not what you want to avoid (how fit you want to become, not how much fat you want to get rid of).

Be as clear and specific as possible ("I will have supper with my family three nights a week" rather than "I will be home earlier") and feel free to enrich and add as much emotion to your affirmation statement as possible. Ideally, when you read it, it should stir up a feeling and make a picture pop into your mind.

For instance, if your goal is to run a full marathon for the first time in your life, your goal statement might look like this:

MY GOAL:

By August 15th of next year,

I am so happy and thankful now that I am able to run a full marathon. My body is in great shape. I look radiant and very healthy and I feel fantastic too. Everybody I speak with says they notice the positive change in me.

This might sound silly, but affirmations like these are the ultimate secret to impressing what you want upon your subconscious mind.

✏   For each of your most important goals, transfer it, in affirmation format, to a goal card. (You may also wish to write a goal statement beneath each "When" in your journal.)

If you have a laminator, you may wish to laminate your goal card for longevity purposes.

Keep your goal cards in front of you—affix them to your wall, desk or computer if you wish—to inspire you to take daily action.

Chapter Twelve

Create an Action Plan

Objectives you wrote and ordered in your journal are the beginnings of your "action plan."

Action plans are lists of responsibilities that instruct a person to carry out elements of short-term goals on a day-to-day basis; they will have a great deal to do with your day-to-day scheduling. Action plans show the minute steps, the individual points between A and Z. They center your attention on the goals immediately needing achievement.

What does an action plan look like?

An action plan is simply a list of the most logical steps you need to take to achieve a short-term goal, in the order you need to take them.

✐   Write an action plan:
1. Choose one of your important long-term goals to work on. Read through each of its short-term goals, beginning with the first one you must carry out, and determine the minute steps you must take to accomplish that goal, in the order you must take them.
2. In your journal (you may wish to begin a new section or a new journal), write in list format the minutes steps you must take, in the order you must take them. This list is your action plan for that goal.
3. If you find it motivates you, include a time frame for accomplishing each step. Be realistic so that you neither over- nor under-challenge yourself.
4. Beginning with the first step of your action plan, carry out your first goal.

5. Check off each minute step you accomplish.
6. Do the same for all your minute and short-term goals, so that you may see the swiftness of your progress toward achieving your dream.

Congratulations! You have learned to focus your effort and energy in order to become a successful goal getter! With just a few more hints, you'll be fully prepared to delve into Part Three where you'll learn how to make the most effective use of your time.

Chapter Thirteen

Why People Fail to Set and Achieve Goals

Despite inspiring dreams, despite energetic and motivating mission and vision statements, people can still fail to set and achieve goals.

But what causes this to happen?

And what remedies will overcome it?

Here are the most common reasons people fail to set and achieve goals, and their remedies:

No perceived need. Review Chapter Two, "Your Current State of Affairs." If you scored yourself 100 percent on all dimensions, there is no need for change. However, I have never met anyone who scored themselves 100 percent on all dimensions. So there must be room for improvement somewhere!

Not enough time. When you are interested you do what is convenient. When you are committed you do whatever it takes. Most people are only interested in dreaming of how life could be. They are not committed to doing whatever it takes to make those dreams a reality. Whether it is completing their planning, getting up early or staying late, they are just not committed. If you choose to simply go about your daily business—not making the time to set goals and fulfill them—then tomorrow will bring you exactly the same as it brought you today. If you do not make time for change, you are cheating yourself out of great opportunities.

Laziness. In the short term, laziness can be considered an exaggeration of the natural instinct to get healthy rest, and conserve precious energy. It isn't something necessarily bad. But it is important to ask yourself if this state of mind and behavior will get you where you would like to be. Is the answer causing you pain or pleasure? Which do you prefer?

Illusion of busyness. Too many interests and activities create an illusion of busyness but with no real focus or direction. Dare to be honest. What is this busyness bringing you in respect to happiness, joy, pleasure? If you have no real focus or direction, you will be moving but getting nowhere.

Wanting to please others. Wanting to please others and always do what you think others want you to do rather than choosing to do what *you* want to do will hinder goal-setting and achievement. There may also be an imbalance in your relationships with others and in the outcome of these relationships. Quite often this wanting to please others will lead to a lose/win situation, with you on the losing end. You might be on your way to losing your own desires or even your own identity. My advice is, take another look at Chapter Two, "Your Current State of Affairs." You may be living an unbalanced life. Ask yourself how this makes you feel. If it does not feel good, it might be time for you to make a change. If you have difficulty breaking this habit and it is causing you trouble, please consider obtaining professional help.

Do not believe in your own ability to design and propel your own life. If this is the case, you might be suffering from a lack of self-confidence. Just about everybody will suffer from a lack of self-confidence sometimes. Having a set of simple exercises you can practice during these times is an invaluable aid to getting your confidence level back on track as quickly as possible.

Here are six actions you can take to boost or maintain your confidence:

1. Don't give yourself a hard time. Don't be your own worst critic—be your own best friend. After all, if a friend of yours was going through a tough time, you would lift him up rather than tear him down. Positive self-talk can be one of your best tools for confidence-boosting, so make sure you cultivate the habit.
2. Remember a time when you felt confident. Confidence is a feeling, and if you've felt it once, you can feel it again. Remembering a time when you felt confident and in control will enable you to reexperience that feeling and help to put you in a confident frame of mind.

3. Practice. Whatever it is you want to feel confident about, practice it as often as you can. When you work on something until you could do it in your sleep, you can't fail to be confident in your ability to perform when it matters.

4. Practice correct posture. This might not sound like it's obviously related to confidence, but how you sit and how you stand sends a message out to those around you. If that message radiates confidence, you will get positive vibes back that will bolster your confidence. So learn to sit and stand like you have confidence.

5. Surround yourself with confident and positive people. It may seem self-evident, but if you are consistently mixing with people of low self-esteem, this is going to rub off on you. Conversely, if the people around you are upbeat and assured, this will create a positive atmosphere that you will benefit from.

6. Think about all the qualities you like about yourself and your talents and abilities. If you have any trouble doing this, think about the compliments you get from people: what do they say you do well? It's a good idea to write these positive characteristics down so you'll have them to refer to when your confidence is flagging and you need some inspiration. Make sure you give yourself due credit for these regularly—this will prove to be the best springboard for building unstoppable confidence.

Negative thinking. Negative thinking includes any thoughts or forms of self-talk that include criticism, doubt, low expectations and put-downs. These thoughts usually stem from our insecurities and are repeated automatically by our subconscious mind many times throughout the day. If left unchallenged, these negative thoughts can lead to lack of motivation, below average performance, self-doubt, and a tendency to fail.

If positive thinking can motivate you to succeed, it's possible that negative thinking can motivate you to fail. If we are capable of achieving anything that we believe, it stands to reason that if we believe we will fail, we can achieve that too.

So how do you beat negative thinking at its own game? The first step is to get to the source of the problem.

Negative thinking has two main origins: internal beliefs and external sources. The internal beliefs stem from any negative feelings that you may be harboring. The external sources can come from any person or event that caused you to become unsure of yourself or your abilities.

Most negative internal beliefs stem from insecurity. These insecurities can be based on events, honest mistakes or, more often, misconceptions. If these events are left unchallenged they can lead to feelings of low self-confidence, low self-esteem, and anxiety. Then, the next time that you experience a negative event, your insecurities use that event as fuel to reinforce the negative thoughts and feed your negative self-talk.

So, how does internal negativity start? There are many causes, but they all share a general theme. Internal negatively stems from the way we react to any given situation.

Internal forces of negative thinking: Fear of what lies beyond your comfort zone. Think back to when you were a child. Most of us have limitations put upon our lives in a very early stage. We are taught how to think, which schools to attend, how to make a living, and finally, even how to plan our retirement. Many of us end up fearing anything that is different from what we were taught.

For us to be able to change the things that we are unhappy with in our lives, we have to change the way that we think and act. If we never change the way that we think and act, we will continue to get the same results.

About ninety percent of people live their lives and never become the person that they dream of becoming. This happens simply because they fail to take action. They fear what they don't understand. We have to look at fear as nothing more than a word or a learning process. Mark Twain said it best with this quote: "Do the things that you fear most and the death to fear is certain." You owe it to yourself to overcome fear.

Begin with the small items that scare you. And gradually tackle the bigger issues. After doing so, you will look back and think how foolish it was to have been afraid in the first place.

Learn to leave your comfort zone. When we leave our comfort zone we become a more rounded individual. When we do the things we fear and look back at them afterward, we see—to our surprise—that what we feared has now turned into part of our comfort zone. The next time similar situations arise we will no longer stress over it, we will just do it.

We must set our minds to always conquer the unknown. Always think outside the box. Look fear in the eyes and just do the task. Every successful person has undoubtedly faced fear many times, yet they have succeeded in their endeavors. So can you.

Internal forces of negative thinking: Fear of not being good enough. This source of negative thinking usually stems from our own misconceptions of how "good" others expect us to be. This misconception usually starts with a well-meaning parent or teacher who pushed you too hard when you were young. While they were most likely only trying to motivate you to always do your best, you may have been doing your best and came away from the experience feeling not good enough. It also comes from people who are judgmental or tear-you-downers. If we believe that others expect us to be perfect at all times, then even the most subtle failure could result in feelings of worthlessness, depression and anxiety.

The main problem with this insecurity is that our belief keeps us from realizing that it isn't others who are holding us to such high standards. This level of perfection is almost always self-imposed.

By harboring this misconception, you force yourself to perform in a constant state of overachievement. While the desire to overachieve can be great at times, it can also take away from your success. Why? Because perfection takes time. If you find yourself spending too much time on each and every decision or project, you could be robbing yourself of the chance to undertake or discover bigger and better opportunities. Also, perfectionists are unintentionally setting themselves up for a fall. No one can be perfect all the time. If you constantly hold yourself to this level of performance, you will eventually be disappointed. And, unfortunately, this disappointment can lead to an increase in negative thinking. So keep this in mind when you take action or plan goals. Often good is plenty good enough.

Internal forces of negative thinking: Fear of making a mistake. The way we react to making a mistake can either strengthen our belief in our problem-solving skills or increase our negative views about ourselves. The difference comes from how we react to those mistakes. If you make a mistake, do you admit to it or do you run from it? Do you view it as a learning experience or as a reason to feel worthless? Do you see it as a just another experience or as an unavoidable happening based on your lack of skills?

If your prior experience with mistakes resulted in shame, then you will naturally harbor a fear of making mistakes. While you may use this fear as a way to protect yourself, it is a form of negative self-talk that can keep you from advancement and achievement. Think about that for a minute. If you are afraid to make a mistake, you will never try anything new, thus keeping yourself from discovering new opportunities and acting on great ideas.

Internal forces of negative thinking: Fear of failure. It is good to realize most successful people have failed miserably. That's right. At one time or another they have flopped, fell short, missed the mark, struck out or goofed up. Beethoven's music teacher once told him that as a composer, he was hopeless. Winston Churchill failed the 6th grade. Albert Einstein failed the entrance exams to the Swiss Polytechnic Institute. J. K. Rowling lived on welfare in an apartment infested with mice. Steven Spielberg dropped out of high school in his sophomore year. He was persuaded to come back and placed in a learning disabled class. He lasted a month and dropped out of school forever. However, the difference between these people and the rest of the world is that when they failed, they made a choice to use the experience to better themselves. They determined to become stronger and to reach their goals.

Are you determined to reach your goal? Do you really believe you can achieve what you set out to accomplish? With determination and belief, you too can make the same choice to turn a failed situation into a winning one. How? By choosing to adapt a positive perspective and engage in edifying self-talk. Here are four phrases you can use to stay motivated when things don't go as you planned or wished them to:

1. "The only direction is up" or "It can't get any worse." Feel like you've hit rock bottom? Don't beat up on yourself too badly. To experience disappointment, heartbreak, embarrassment or self-doubt is to be human. However, to wallow in this state for too long is downright destructive. Tell yourself that it doesn't get much worse than this point, and let yourself know that the only place left to go is upward. Use failure as motivation to start climbing back up. When you do this, you will see that instead of running from failure, you will look it in the eye and overcome it.

2. "This is not the end of the line." Know this: everyone fails from time to time but failure is not the end of the line unless you allow it to be. You tried, you blundered, you failed and it hurts. Allow yourself time to grieve it, but then let it go so that you can get back to the business of reaching your intended goal. Remind yourself that the only positive option is to seek ways to turn the situation around. Then tell yourself that in the morning you will begin again!

3. "Hmmm, I may need to change direction." Does it seem like you've come to a roadblock? Then the solution may just be detouring and moving toward your goal in a different way. When something does not work out as planned, you may need to reevaluate the route you are taking. So review the situation, regroup, and get on a track

around that roadblock. The track may be a different one, but it may also be a more successful one.

4. "I'll do better next time." As long as you're breathing, there's always room for improvement. Choose to use your failure as positive motivation to do better the next time around. When you remember your goal and envision reaching it, you will be super-charged to find ways to develop yourself. For example, if you need to do better in school, make (and follow) a consistent study schedule. If you are intent on a promotion at work, take classes to increase your skill set. No matter what the failed task consists of, you can use it to motivate yourself to get more done.

Internal forces of negative thinking: Fear of not being able to change. A few lucky people do realize the reasons behind their negative thinking. However, they fail to recognize that these reasons can be changed. "I have never been any good at this kind of thing." "That's just the way I am." "I can't help how I think or feel." Do any of these statements sound familiar? These self-limiting statements stem from a fear of being unable to change. The statements afford us an excuse for our behavior. After all, if it can't be helped, then it can't be our fault.

The problem with these statements is that they limit us from achieving our true potential. If we believe the statements when we think them, then our reactions to them are almost always self-fulfilling. With these negative thoughts running through our minds, we are unable to accomplish certain goals even if we want to.

Internal forces of negative thinking: Fear of success. Fear of success may sound like a strange idea, but many people can identify with the feelings below:
* Do you ever feel like something is holding you back?
* Do you find that you "get in your own way"?
* Do you feel real achievement is constantly just out of your grasp?

Now consider the positives and negatives you associate to being successful. For example, many people have the following associations to being successful:
* "If I became financially successful I might not be spiritual."
* "If I became successful I might lose my family."
* "If I became successful I might have a lot more pressure on me to perform, as well as a lot more pressure on my time, and I might not have time to do what I want to do."

This fear of success can result in:

- Losing the motivation or the desire to grow, achieve, and succeed
- A lack of effort to achieve goals you have set for yourself in school, on the job, at home, in relationships, or in your personal growth
- Problems making decisions, being unable to solve problems
- Chronic underachievement
- Self-destructive behavior: tripping yourself up to make sure you do not keep a certain level of success or achievement you once had in school, on the job, at home, in relationships, or in your personal growth
- Feeling guilt, confusion, and anxiety when you do achieve success. This leads you to falter, waver, and eventually lose your momentum

Fear of success is all about conflicting beliefs. In the event of conflicting beliefs, the stronger ones will always override the weaker ones. It is your dominant beliefs that have the true authority over your reality creation.

We know that conflicting beliefs can be a source of self-sabotage. But conflicting beliefs may only slow you down and not entirely stop you from achieving success. Whether self-sabotage kills you or not depends on the collective strength of your empowering beliefs against that of your disempowering ones.

The more harmonious beliefs you have and the less conflicting ones, the faster you will be able to achieve success in the area that those beliefs have relevance to.

External forces of negative thinking. Now that we have identified the internal sources of negative thinking, let's examine the external sources. These sources can be easier to recognize but a little harder to control. Nevertheless it's good to know what you may run into as you begin your goal-setting career.

External sources of negative thinking come from outside ourselves but their true harm comes from the way we react to these sources.

Think about this for a minute. We cannot always control what happens to us, or the people we meet, but we can control how we react to each of these events.

For example, if you are thinking about introducing a new product to your business but everyone you share the idea with has a negative opinion about it, your reaction may be to second-guess your idea.

Or, if you are about to undertake a new exercise program, but your spouse comments that you will never stick with it, your subconscious may believe him or her and your reaction may be to lose your motivation.

While those examples show how another person's comments can induce negative thinking, events can also have the same effect. Say, for example, that you did introduce a new product but it didn't sell well. The event could play on your insecurities and your reaction might be to think negatively about yourself and your business abilities.

Or, if you started an exercise program but didn't see the results that you wanted, your reaction might be to fall into a trap of thinking it was your fault. Your insecurities could cause you to think, "I knew I couldn't do it" or "Nothing I ever do turns out right."

Events that are even farther beyond your control can also be a source of negative thinking. For instance, if you were laid off from your job because of downsizing, negative thoughts can begin to form from that event. Although the layoff had nothing to do with you or your abilities personally, the event can still lead you to form a negative opinion about yourself. One scenario would be to decide that you were cursed with bad luck. If you were to continue believing this, then you might shy away from new opportunities or automatically talk yourself into failing at your next job.

As you can see, each of these sources or insecurities can lead to negative thinking. The key is to learn to recognize these insecurities. Recognizing insecurities and knowing that they are very common makes it easier to cope with them before they stop you from achieving what you want.

Beliefs. Beliefs are the various ideas you think are true and use as a basis for daily action. Beliefs can be both permissive and limiting. Your beliefs create your reality. The trick to success is to know your current beliefs and how they affect you so you can then select beliefs that will support the life you wish for.

Beliefs are the assumptions we make about ourselves and about others. Beliefs are about how we think things really are, what we think is really true, and what we therefore expect as likely consequences that will follow from our behavior.

When a person owns a belief, he or she consciously accepts their belief. This can vary from mild acceptance to confident absoluteness. Thus it would prove meaningless to say that a person has beliefs without them knowing it, or for them to deny their own beliefs. Obviously, a person who does not believe in something does not believe in that something; a person who believes in something, does believe in that something. Belief requires conscious acceptance.

The term "limiting belief" is used for a belief that inhibits exploration of a wider cognitive space than would otherwise be the case. A limiting belief holds us back. Examples of limiting beliefs are seen both in animals and people. These may be strongly held beliefs and are often tied in with self-image or perceptions about the world. Here are a few everyday examples of limiting beliefs:

- That one has specific capabilities, roles, or traits that cannot be escaped or changed
- That one cannot succeed so there is no point committing to trying
- That a particular opinion is right therefore there is no point considering other viewpoints
- That a particular action or result is the only way to resolve a problem

If you think you have limiting beliefs that could sabotage reaching your goals, it would be wise to work on them through counseling.

Obstacles to "Why." Just as you considered the most important benefits you will receive by reaching your goal (chapter 8), you also need to consider the most important obstacles you could encounter in your journey toward goal completion.

It's not a question of whether you will have roadblocks; it's a question of what and when, and whether or not you will prevail. That's why your "Why" must be strong—to take you through those challenges so you can reach your goals.

Obstacles, as we just learned, can be internal (coming from your limiting beliefs, doubts or fears) or external (caused by events or people). Here's how to make the distinction. Ask yourself:

- "What past conditioning and old beliefs are standing in my way?"
- "What am I saying to me that is standing in my way?"

If appropriate, you might benefit from consulting with a certified practitioner who specializes in helping people to clear old limiting beliefs, hurtful past events, and negative conditioning.

🖊 In your journal, list every obstacle you can think of that could stop you from achieving each goal. For example: no time to cook better food, too heavy of a schedule, drop-in visitors, procrastination, improper scheduling, lack of discipline, unexpected work requirements, friends expect me to drink with them, bad eating habits.

Now list insights you discovered in this chapter that might help you to get around, or to overcome, those obstacles.

Chapter Fourteen

Habits that Bring Success

Successful people form positive habits to accomplish things less successful people don't like to do. Which of your habits will bring success? Which of your habits should you change to achieve the success you deserve?

✎ In the following self-test, check each habit as it currently applies to you. (Note: A positive mental attitude is usually behind a successful habit. And remember, it takes courage to accept the truth.)

Habits that bring success	Currently Follow	Intend to Follow
Do you have a clear sense of purpose or direction for your life?	√	√
Are you able to stay focused and concentrate all your efforts onto one definite aim?	√	√
Are you usually able to make decisions and work consistently on them?	√	√
Are you willing to take a chance on a positive outcome even if it is risky?	√	√
Are you willing to do whatever it takes to achieve your goals?	√	√
Do you control your negative thoughts?	√	√

Do you practice good habits which contribute to your good health: nutritious moderate diet, regular exercise, physical and mental relaxation?	√	√
Can you persist in the face of difficulty? (When the going gets tough, many people give up.)	√	√
Are you willing to aim high? (Many people put up with average goals and mediocre performance.)	√	√
Do you seek out and surround yourself with people who encourage and coach you to great success? (Too many people listen to those who say "you can't.")	√	√
Are you willing to learn, read, and pick up the knowledge and skills to make you a generalist (able to adapt to and succeed in almost any environment)? (People who become too specialized become white elephants who cannot keep up with the speed of changes in our society.)	√	√
Are you enthusiastic, committed and motivated?	√	√
Do you make things happen for you? (Victims wait for things to happen to them.)	√	√

Table 1: Habits that bring success

✎   What are you going to do about the successful habits that do not yet apply to you?

Chapter Fifteen

Character Matters

No amount of wealth can compensate for a lack of character. Character equals integrity and integrity means you do what is right—even when no one is watching you.

In a practical sense, this means you practice the golden rule by doing to others as you would have them do to you. In your daily life, there are many opportunities for you to make this rule a part of your routine. Think about it. Have you ever been tempted to shortcut your way to the top of the corporate ladder? Reaching this goal is a wonderful achievement, but take a look around you. Are the hallways in your office building stacked high with the bodies of people you stepped on to get there? If so, be prepared to get stepped on in return.

Do you routinely treat people with honesty and respect? Or do you have a short temper when it comes to dealing with people who refuse to bow down to your every wish and command? The person with character and integrity will never have to worry about this because they know that no one achieves success single-handedly. Whether it's success in the business world, in sports or raising a family, someone was probably there to offer a helping hand along the way. The person with character and integrity will know and appreciate this and offer the same helping hand when the opportunity arises.

Celebrated portrait photographer, Yousuf Karsh, was famous for photographing celebrities and world leaders. He said, "I have found that great people do have in common a great belief in themselves and their mission. They also have great determination as well as an ability to work hard. At the crucial moment of decision, they draw on their accumulated wisdom. Above all, they have integrity."

It is important that you take a good look at your attitude regarding what success means to you. Albert Einstein said, "Weakness of attitude becomes weakness of character."

Character is what you are. Success is what you achieve. What you achieve can be large or small, but success without character and integrity is merely a shadow. Your character matters as you work toward your goals, and it is a quality you will pass on to your children. So let your strength of character shine through in all you do and say and you will be able to achieve great successes.

Chapter Sixteen

Goal Setting: Final Insights

We began this book with the dreams we wanted to set goals to achieve and the aspects of ourselves we wanted to set goals to improve. Then we wrote mission and vision statements, then solidified and wrote our goals, taking into consideration "Who," "What," "Why," "How," and "When." We used this process to explain the goal setting process from an educational point of view, keeping the steps simple and clear.

Outside the classroom we sometimes work differently. The human brain doesn't always use a chronological or hierarchic approach. It often uses a more indefinable approach. This means it might come up with a goal statement first before even considering the obstacles or the role. The next time it might use an unsatisfied role and search for a goal and benefits to satisfy it. In other words, every goal might originate from a different place. Feel free to let them. Just remember it is important that you give all elements consideration when you choose a new goal.

Our education system focuses on filling our heads with data, facts, and figures. The learner is often passive. Goal setting requires assessment and problem solving skills. Goal setting involves application and organization. The learner is active and requires original thinking, lateral thoughts, personal independence, and responsibility.

Goal setting is a formal process for personal planning. By setting goals on a routine basis you will decide what you want to achieve, and then, step by step, you will move toward achieving those goals.

Goals are what will keep you motivated and focused—both essential to being productive. Think of goals and aims as necessary achievements. In achieving your desired goals, you should start with a positive outlook. You must be excited with the challenges and tasks that you have to do to give you the right start or motivation. As you proceed on the roadmap to success and happiness, just be sure to keep your goals realistic; do not try to do everything at once. You can't drive to two different cities at once; neither should you try to accomplish too many goals at once or you will find yourself feeling pulled apart and overwhelmed.

How many long-term goals should you be working on? Three or four, maximum. If you attempt more it will become increasingly difficult to make time for good quality actions to achieve those goals.

For each new, future goal, I recommend you work through the goal setting process outlined in Parts One and Two of this book, until you have worked through the process a few times and are comfortable with it. This will take some time and will force you to fully concentrate on all the elements of successful goal setting. It's like Confucius said, "I see, I forget. I hear, I remember. I do, I understand." You have to do it to understand how it works and to master it. Once you have mastered it you will be able to enjoy it and reap the benefits.

As you get more experienced you might be able to skip some steps. Especially when your goals have common denominators. After all, you can always work through the entire process when you are thinking of planning a goal in a territory you are not familiar with.

Hold on to your journal. On days when the going gets tough, and your enthusiasm for goal setting wears thin, your journal will be there to remind you what it's all about. Your mission and vision statements are there, as are your dreams. You have recorded them, to enable you to move forward, and so you can read them on a rainy day.

If you commit to your written goals and are diligent, you are half way to accomplishing happiness and success.

In Conclusion

People who set goals and follow up on them are usually better capable living their life to the fullest.

Just think of time you set a goal and steadily worked toward it to ultimate success: the thrill of losing weight, completing a marathon, planning a great wedding to look back on, starting a home-based business, saving money or earning a college degree, and feeling fulfilled and happy with your achievements.

How many of the following applied to you then:

- Steadily moving toward and achieving the results you want by losing a pound each week
- Clear and focused direction giving you a sense of accomplishment and purpose when you trained for the marathon
- High enthusiasm for what you had in mind as you planned your wedding
- Boosted self-esteem, confidence and belief in your ability to make it happen and feeling in control by finally saving money instead of getting into debt
- Efficient and effective use of your time preparing for your exam

These are just a few of the many benefits you will reap from your newfound knowledge of goal-setting. If you struggled on the last point, "Efficient and effective use of your time preparing for your exam" or on any goal you set out to achieve that involved time, have no worries. In the next section, Part Three: Time Management, you'll learn secrets to make the best use of your time, to bring you success, happiness, and realization of your goals and dreams.

Keep in mind:

60% of people do not set goals.

10% of people set goals, but do not write them down.

3% of people set goals and write them down *and* act . . .

and the 3% does 50 times better than all the others put together!

Welcome to the 3% Club.

PART THREE: Time Management

Chapter Seventeen

What Is Time Management?

Benjamin Franklin said, "Do you love life? Then do not squander time, for that's the stuff that life is made of."

Time, like oil, is a nonrenewable resource and is also incredibly easy to burn. Time is a unique resource because you get the same amount as everyone else. Once it's gone, you can never get it back.

One thing that you can do with your time is change the way you use it.

So what is time management?

Time management, simply put, is about making choices. Good choices lead to better results, while poor choices lead to wasted time and energy. It isn't just about having time; it's about making sure your time is well spent.

Time management includes tools, or techniques and skills, for effectively planning and scheduling time. When you effectively plan and schedule your time, you will be better able to reach your dreams and goals.

There are unfortunately many erroneous assumptions regarding time management. A number of them may even sound familiar:

- "There is never enough time to do what is important."
  This is wrong. There is always enough time to carry out what is essential.
- "Other people make too many demands on my time."
  Although this may feel so, other people do not control how you spend your time. You do. If you allow other people to lay too many claims on your time, they will continue to do so.

- "Given my busy schedule, it's impossible for me to work based on priorities."
  It is not only possible, it's essential. To control your time, you must set priorities and stick to them.
- "If you want something done right, do it yourself."
  This assumption stems from asking yourself the wrong question: "Can I do this task better than anyone else?" Instead, ask yourself: "Is this task the best use of my time? Could someone else do this task well enough?"
- "If only I could work more hours every day, I could complete what I need to do."
  This one is not only wrong, it is dangerous. Working more hours every day produces mental and physical fatigue and devours personal time. You can't do everything; learn to set priorities and make some choices. In other words, work smarter, not longer.
- "I'm often overworked in my job."
  Sure, that's possible, but it's more likely that you are suffering from an inability to say no, to set priorities, or delegate.
- "I'm much too busy to plan my activities."
  The busier you are, the more important it becomes that you take time out to plan. Planning is one of the main keys to time management.
- "I should stick to my plan for the day no matter what happens."
  In the real world, the unexpected and unplanned have a way of cropping up. But when the unexpected does occur, ask yourself: "Is this more important than what I had planned to do?" If it isn't, don't do it.
- "Time management will make me inflexible."
  Turning down your boss's urgent assignment by saying, "I have a strict schedule to follow and tomorrow is my filing day so I cannot accept another assignment now," will certainly get you into trouble. When you are asked to help out with some backed-up invoicing, you can decide if giving a helpful hand to an important part of the business will improve your reputation as a team player. Or if it will cause other, equally important jobs that have already been assigned to you to become delayed or risked.

  Flexibility implies that you can still make last-minute decisions. When you have an eleventh-hour invitation out for a couples-only supper on Friday night, you can decide if one more social gathering will contribute to your happiness as a couple. Or if it will drain you for the family affairs you already booked up for the weekend.

Making conscious decisions about why we use the time the way we do will prevent you from appearing incapable or feeling overwhelmed. You will have the confidence to give your answer yes or no without later questioning your judgment.

When you set up a good time management routine, you are growing and upholding a personal commitment to yourself, with the ability to be more flexible than ever before.

Time management is not a device to make you work harder and longer. Far from it. It is a means to help you work smarter to accomplish more in less time with greater results.

Chapter Eighteen

Your Current State of Affairs

Here's an easy self-test to find out how well your time-management skills are currently developed.

For each of the questions below, give yourself 3, 2, 1, or 0 points, according to the following scoring key:

- If your answer is "always," give yourself 3 points.
- If your answer is "usually," give yourself 2 points.
- If your answer is "occasionally," give yourself 1 point.
- If your answer is "rarely" or "never," give yourself 0 points.

Question	Score
Do you think about and plan your day before you start it?	
Do you write appointments and key tasks in your calendar?	
Do you keep—and use—a continuing "to do" list?	
Do you use this "to do" list as a reminder of things you would like to do in the future?	
Do you group similar tasks together and do them consecutively?	
Do you use waiting time to handle small tasks?	
Do you handle the most important tasks of the day when you feel most alert?	
Do you stop working on a task when you begin to feel stressed or overwhelmed?	
Do you feel your personal life and professional life are well balanced?	

Do you keep a simple but well-defined filing system into which you place all loose papers and materials?	
Do you organize your work tools, such as pens, rulers, phone and computer so they are ready to use the minute you want them?	
When you enter your office or pick up your mail, do you immediately discard messages and items you don't need?	
Do you keep reference materials, such as telephone books, rolodexes, and important manuals within arm's reach of your primary work area?	
Do you have a specific time allotted each day to handle memos, messages, and correspondence?	
Do you shut your door or engage in quiet time when you must handle detail work?	
Do you keep a simple time log to systematically access where and how you spend your time?	
Do you have a good insight in the values you live by?	
Do you regularly review 90-day goals for your personal and professional life?	
Do you take time each week to appraise your productivity and discover whether you have completed the goals you set out to accomplish?	
Total your points	

Table 2: Your current state of affairs

If you score ranges between 50 and 60, congratulations! You are nearing perfection. There's still room for some improvement though. The following chapters will help you to top things off.

If your score ranges between 40 and 49, good. With some modest improvements in your time-management habits, you can become even more productive each day. After completion of this book you will be able to achieve your goals quickly and have more time for yourself.

If your score ranges between 30 and 39, you're on the right track. You need to make a few easy changes that will enable you to accomplish more and free up time as well. This book will serve as your guide.

If your score is below 25, you've definitely come to the right place. The following chapters can dramatically help you to improve your time management skills and achieve far more than you ever thought possible.

This self-test gave you an indication of how you are currently managing your time. Feel free to take the test again over the coming months so that you can track—and enjoy watching—your progress.

Chapter Nineteen

Activity Logs

A method you can use to get more detailed insight into how you are using your time is an activity log.

An activity log is simply a page or two in your journal where you note how you spend a day's time. When you first use an activity log you may be shocked to see the time you waste! Memory is a poor guide when it comes to this, as it can be too easy to forget time spent on non-core tasks. Do you know how much time you spend reading junk mail? Talking to colleagues? Making coffee? Eating lunch? Doing the laundry? Or fetching a missing ingredient at the grocery store?

Activity logs can also help you to track changes in your energy, alertness and effectiveness throughout the day. Most people find they work at different levels of effectiveness at different times of day as their energy levels vary. Your effectiveness may vary depending on: the amount of sugar in your blood, the length of time since you last took a break, routine distractions, stress, discomfort, or other causes.

✎   Keep an activity log for two days to better understand how you spend your time and when you perform at your best. Choose two days which you would consider to be normal days. In your journal, log your activities, the importance or value of that activity, and how you feel throughout each day. List the start times of each activity and write down a new start time each time you change activities.

Here is an example of an activity log:

Activity Log				
Time	Activity description	Duration	Value (high, medium, low)	How I feel
8:05	prepare breakfast	20	high	tired
8:25	read newspaper	10	medium	tired
8:35	drive to work	35	high	flat
9:10	fetch coffee + greet coworkers	10	low	flat
9:20	open + check mail + start computer	5	medium	flat
9:25	interruption coworker	10	low	flat
9:35	check mail	5	medium	flat
9:40	start working on important report	10	high	alert
9:50	telephone interruption	10	low	flat

Table 3: Activity log

While you do not have to state your mood for each activity, try to establish a pattern by listing at least every hour how you feel: alert, flat, tired, energetic, and so on. The more detailed your log, the easier it will be to see patterns emerge.

✐ After two days, analyze your daily activity log. You may be alarmed to see the amount of time you waste doing low-value jobs.

You may also notice that you feel energetic in particular parts of the day, and flat in other parts. Much of this can depend on the rest breaks you take, the times and amounts you eat, and quality of your nutrition.

Also take into consideration the energy drainers and energy gainers. Could an energy drainer or gainer be something you ate? A conversation you had? Something you did? An interruption? The activity log gives you a basis for experimenting with these variables.

Understand your peak times. If you are a morning person, get up at the crack of dawn and get jobs done. Recognize your most productive times, and schedule your most important tasks within those times.

Your analysis should help you determine time you can free up during your day. Gain that extra time by applying one of the following actions to as many time-wasting activities as possible:

- Reduce the time spent on legitimate personal activities such as making coffee. Take turns with your team member to do this—it saves time and strengthens team spirit.
- Try to lessen the number of times a day you switch between kinds of tasks. For example, read and reply to e-mails in blocks only once in the morning and once in the afternoon.
- Schedule your most challenging tasks for the times of day when your energy is highest. That way your work will be better and it should take you less time.
- Cut out jobs that your employer shouldn't be paying you to do. These may include tasks that someone else in the organization should be doing, possibly at a lower pay rate, or personal activities such as sending non-work e-mails.

Chapter Twenty

The Monetary Value of Your Time

In the preceding chapter you gained insight into the way you spend your time, and your energy levels during the day.

While every dollar has the same value, every hour does not. An hour at ten to eleven o'clock in the morning may be of much more value as a working hour than ten to eleven o'clock at night. On the other hand, an hour at your child's bedside when he is ill is worth more than an hour at the office catching up on e-mails.

Understanding the monetary value of time can lead you to appreciate, and wisely invest, the time you have available.

There are two ways to measure the dollar value of your time. You can look at it from an employer point of view and from your own perspective.

1. **What does an hour cost your employer?**

   If you work for someone, you cost the business more than just your hourly wage.

   ✎   Calculate the following, estimating the expense of any unknowns per month: your wage, benefits, office space, equipment, and any other significant costs particular to your job. Divide the total amount by the hours you work in a month. The resulting figure is how much an hour costs your employer.

   For example, your monthly salary might be $3000. Add 30 percent for cost of office space and other costs. Now we're up to $3900. Divide this by the number of hours you work in an average month. If you work 100 hours a month you will cost your employer

$39 per hour. If you are known to waste time and haven't received a raise or a bonus, this may be why.

The next time you consider whether to undertake an activity, you can determine if the task is worth the amount your time and other physical resources would cost the business.

What if you cost your business $5 per minute instead of $5 per hour? Or $10 per minute instead of $10 per hour? Would you hang around an office waiting room, or stay on hold on the telephone? Or would you confirm appointments and leave messages?

2. **What does an hour cost you?**

Are you self-employed or do you work on contract? This makes it essential that you spend your time wisely or wasted time may have an immediate impact on your income.

🖊 Create a list of necessary business activities that do not directly produce income, such as contacting prospective clients, bookkeeping, Web site maintenance, and cleaning. Based on the previous month, estimate the number of hours you spent doing each task. The following chart will serve as an example:

Non-income-producing activities	Hours spent per month
Contacting prospective clients	12
Bookkeeping	8
Web site maintenance	15
Cleaning	10

Table 4: Non-income-producing activities

🖊 How much do you currently charge per billing hour? If you bill $30 per hour for your service and you spend fifteen hours per month maintaining your Web site, the task has cost you $450 that month.

It may alternatively have cost you fifteen hours away from your family and friends, or impeded on production time. If having an up-to-date Web site is important to your business (but is not the actual business), then perhaps you would do better to pay someone to maintain it for you. It will give you more time for important tasks and may be carried out in less time if the person is more skilled than you are.

The value of your time: Beyond money

Time management goes beyond recognizing the monetary value of your time. Your personal time also has value.

Your existence is made up of people, interests, and caring for yourself and others. Basing your time solely on the money you will either make or save is missing the big picture.

When your child has a school event he wants you to attend, or when you haven't spent one evening all week to rest and relax, you need to determine the value of your time in the context of living a fulfilling life, not just making money.

If you had six months to live, what would you do? Well? What *would* you do?

Unless they had nagging financial concerns about their family, most people would admit that time spent bettering oneself, spent with family, and showing interest in others has great value.

Chapter Twenty-one

Use Your Personal Prime Time

Learning time management is easier than you may think. In grade school we learned tactics that helped us reach simple goals. From our parents we learned basic time management. If you feel you are running a tight shift, it simply means that it is time to learn extra skills to get ahead.

The first new skill? Use your personal prime time.

Successful time management starts with: making the most of your time! To do so we must make a distinction between prime time and availability time.

Prime time

Your prime time, which you may have discovered with the use of your activity log, is the time during which you are most energetic and efficient. If you haven't yet discovered your prime time answer these questions: At what hours of the day do I work best? When do I achieve the greatest results?

We function on different biological clocks. Some people feel most energetic and do their best work early in the morning. Others wake up and get moving slowly, with top efficiency in the late afternoon. Still others are night owls who perform their work most easily in the middle of the night.

So now that you know your prime time, how do you make the most of it?

Plan to spend it on your creative thinking and most demanding jobs whenever possible. Doing so will enable you excel at your most important tasks, and allow you to accomplish it as quickly as possible.

Availability time

Your availability time is when you need to be available to be with others. For example, busy executives must schedule time to meet with office personnel, managers, production workers, and others under their supervision.

✎ To make the most of your prime time, schedule your availability time around your periods of top efficiency.

Chapter Twenty-two

Eliminate Your Energy Drainers

Another benefit of gaining insight in your energy level fluctuation is that it will enable you to discover energy drainers and eliminate them.

✎ In your journal, log your *emotional* energy for one day (an example follows). Try to identify what causes your emotional energy to remain level, what causes your emotional energy to fall, and what causes your emotional energy to rise. When your emotional energy is between two levels, try to identify where the strongest energy is. This log will enable you to pinpoint emotional energy drainers.

Time	Energy Level	Causes
09:00-11:00	High	I feel in shape and confidant.
11:00-13:00	High – Middle	I still feel good but also a little annoyed because of many interruptions.
13:00-15:00	Low	I feel ashamed because I failed an important exam.
15:00-17:00	Middle	I slowly realized I did not pay enough attention preparing for the exam and I am confident I will pass next time. Plus I have great plans for tonight.

Table 5: Energy level survey

Most of us spend most of our time in the middle energy level. In this example the many interruptions between 11:00-13:00, and the fact that the energy level reported is slipping could be an indication that interruptions drain your energy.

This log shows us temporary emotional energy drainers. But what if instead it revealed a persistent energy level? That is our true concern in this chapter.

Following are three persistent emotional energy levels to be aware of. The first two are energy drainers.

Persistent Low Emotional Energy

When your energy continuously runs low over longer periods of time, there are usually multiple issues and problems causing this. For instance, you might be experiencing feelings of shame, apathy or grief. These feelings can be serious energy drainers.

Shame often leads to self-sabotaging behavior.

Apathy is a state of helplessness where external energy is sought from caregivers. People acting at this level are often felt to be a burden by those around them, as they are needy and may endlessly discuss their problems.

Grief is a feeling everyone experiences for short amounts of time during their life. However, people who grieve for extended periods and continually act within this level live a life of regret and depression.

Grief also is the energy level of habitual losers, who accept failure as part of their lifestyle.

Persistent low emotions are significant energy drainers. If you find yourself stuck in a state of low energy level you might want to consider help from others to tackle the issues that might be holding you back.

Persistent Middle Emotional Energy

It is possible for people to have successful lives operating at predominately middle emotional energy levels. These levels, however, have their own particular concerns, such as feelings of fear, desire, anger, and pride.

As you probably know, fear can be a healthy emotion, as it protects us from danger. As a life-view or continual state of being, however, it can lead to jealousy, chronically high stress, or a fear of success. Fear also can limit personality growth because much energy is spent on dealing with fears.

The desire for money or power dictates the lives of many people and helps to drive the economy. Desire also is the emotional energy level of addictions, where craving becomes more important than outcome of having that addictive craving. Unfortunately, as one desire is achieved, another often quickly replaces it.

Anger can cause people to leave problem situations or deal with them. But as a lifestyle, anger expresses itself as resentment or revenge. Angry people are irritable and explosive, can easily fall into rage, and tend to distance people from themselves.

People feel positive as they reach the level of pride, as they have accomplishment in their lives. However, if pride originates only from external forces, the inflated ego is vulnerable to attack. Also, if a loss of status occurs regarding pride, this energetic level can quickly move to shame.

Persistent High Emotional Energy

The last group of emotional levels signifies the beginning of a crossover point, where power rather than force is used to make decisions and create change. At this level, there is a realization that your own empowerment and the empowerment of others are the true keys to long-term success. This level includes courage, neutrality, willingness, and acceptance.

Courage begins the process of empowerment and the ability to cope and handle the opportunities of life. Courage brings out the capacity to face fear and the capacity to face our own character defects and grow despite them. This is where the world is no longer viewed as black and white. The world starts to look exciting, challenging, and stimulating.

To people of courage, not getting one's way is no longer experienced as defeating or frustrating. Their view is, "If I didn't get this, then I'll get something else. Life has its ups and downs and I will be okay if I roll with the punches." People at this level are easy to get along with and are not interested in conflict.

People who have reached the level of willingness are genuinely friendly and social, and economic success is a part of their lives. They have the ability to overcome inner resistance and do not have any major learning blocks. Having let go of pride, they are willing to look at their own defects and learn from others.

Acceptance is the level where there is the realization that the source of happiness is within oneself. "Love is not something that is given or taken away by another, but is created from within." Long-term goals take precedence over short-term goals. Self-discipline and understanding are prominent.

As mentioned above, if you notice yourself experiencing low energy levels too often it might be the right time to address issues that could be causing you emotional exhaustion.

🖎 If you have a persistent low or middle emotional energy level, set a goal to learn more about your emotional level, then set another goal to lift yourself to a higher level. By doing so you will eliminate debilitating energy drainers and have more time—and better quality time—with which to achieve, succeed, and excel.

Being able to define the important areas of your being, and to take control of the way your life is spent, is a potent energy booster in itself.

Chapter Twenty-three

Focus on Your Strengths

Another commonality among people who successfully manage their time is they focus on their strong traits.

How many times do "well-meaning" managers, colleagues, friends and others advise you to "work on your weaknesses"?

Often, working on your weaknesses is the worst thing you can do!

Now I'm not talking about picking up certain skills or knowledge you currently lack. If you need certain skills or knowledge to achieve a particular goal, then get that skill or knowledge.

What I'm talking about is being consistently "bad" at something, or finding it difficult to master something . . . no matter how hard you try.

Like math. Or writing. Or being neat.

Good news: You're not good at everything and you never will be, so you can quit wasting time trying. You are unique, with unique talents and abilities.

You have *character* strengths—are you upbeat? optimistic? kind? devoted? determined? You also have *ability* strengths (natural abilities)—are you a strong competitor? creative? innovative? a logistical thinker? a problem solver? a singer? an athlete? a musician? You have talents (learned abilities)—are you a gardener? a pilot? a writer? a chef? a computer programmer? a craftsman? an artist? Enjoy yourself for who you are.

Someone musically inept should probably not strive to be the next Yanni.

So are you going to waste precious time and effort struggling to get just a tiny bit better at something that just doesn't—and will never—come naturally, or are you going to build and capitalize on your true talents?

Fact is, you'll gain far, far, far greater value—however you measure that term (money, results, accomplishments, or another measurement), not to mention enjoyment—by improving your strengths.

✎   Go to a place where you will not be disturbed. Take some time to focus on your strengths. In your journal, list your character strengths, ability strengths, and talents. List as many as you can think of—don't be humble, don't be modest. Celebrate the uniqueness of you.

Which of these strengths will benefit you as you move toward achievement of your goals? Struggling to excel at traits that are just not you is waste of time. Forget about them. Instead, work to excel at your strengths.

Chapter Twenty-four

How Your Personality Comes into Play

In the previous chapter we saw we should not invest time trying to develop character traits and abilities that are just not us. We should, however, invest time developing character traits and abilities that are within reach. Especially if doing so will better equip us to accomplish our goals.

In the previous chapter we focused on character traits. In this chapter, we'll put those traits together and focus on personality types.

Learning who we are and what we want is essential for everything we do in life. If we don't understand who we are, we are missing a basic ingredient in ourselves, and in learning what it takes to manage our time wisely.

For our purposes, we will look at two main personality types.

Type A and Type M behavior

Several decades ago, a group of researchers noticed certain psychological patterns in people who were prone to disease, especially heart disease. They labeled the syndrome "Type A" behavior.

Since then, a great deal more has been learned about Type A behavior, including that such behavior is not as simple as people once believed. One lasting insight emerged though: that aggressive, hostile reactions to threats—perceived or actual—are at the core of Type A behavior.

Many of the satellite tendencies of a Type A personality have to do with time. Type A people set unreasonable schedules for themselves and for others. They set up impossible or inappropriate goals. They cram everything into the last minute. They have little time for friends. And, interestingly, even though they seem in constant, frantic activity, they rarely get anything done. Type As boast of their frenzied carryings-on, seek out your sympathy, or try to impose their style on you. They're prophets of doom.

On the other hand, there are people who are almost the opposite of a Type A. Let's call them Type M.

They're quiet but commanding achievers. Their goals are reasonable, their schedules balanced, their dispositions even-tempered.

Colleagues and friends admire them for getting things done. And they seem to suffer less from the recurring ills that plague the classic Type A. Consider the differences in their behavior:

Type A	Type M
Unreasonable schedules	Reasonable schedules
Unreasonable goals	Reasonable goals
Cramming behavior	Long-range planning
Aggressive, hostile	Relaxed, understanding
Mostly acquaintances	True friends
Often ill	Generally healthy
Frantic activity	Steady achievement
Rarely get things done	Get things done

Table 6: Type A and Type M behaviors

The bottom line: you should strive to replace as many Type A traits as you can with Type M ones. It's the reasonable—and healthy—thing to do. You are learning how to change several type A traits in type M traits throughout this book. Some traits, however, you might have to tackle by using self help programs or professional help.

Chapter Twenty-five

Beat Procrastination

Procrastination is simply the habit of putting off for tomorrow what you can do today. When people procrastinate, they are usually putting off doing something that will be a benefit, but for some reason there is more energy put forth to put off the task than to do it. This is a bad habit and is one reason many people do not achieve their dreams.

The fact is that nine out of ten of us have this habit. We tend to postpone jobs and tasks.

Procrastination has at least five negative effects:

- The feeling that a job has been left undone is bad for our morale.
- Unfinished jobs leave a lot of clutter around which affects our efficiency.
- Putting things off means accumulating jobs and urgency could crop up on the same day.
- Procrastination, when it comes to the notice of other people, may be branded as laziness and lack of interest in the job.
- The job becomes more unpleasant the more you postpone it.

Procrastination: Causes and remedies

Following are several causes of—and solutions for—procrastination.

- **Cause:** You're having trouble getting started.
  Solution: Give yourself one tiny task to get your momentum going. Once you get started you will find out that you won't mind doing more than you planned! Let's say your goal is to lose weight and you

decided to work out every day for thirty minutes, but you just can't make yourself do it. So do *one* exercise: "Lift hand weights ten times." Yes, just one exercise, just ten times. It would take you about a minute. Once you get started you're more likely to finish the whole thirty-minute workout!

- **Cause:** The task is too complex. You're paralyzed and overwhelmed.
  Solution: Break the task down into manageable pieces. Can you handle a half-hour task better than you can a four-hour task? Break your four-hour task into eight half-hour tasks, then focus on one half-hour task at a time.

- **Cause:** You hate the task. If the task is boring, or monotonous, or involves too much hard work, then it stands a good chance of getting postponed.
  Solution: Use one or both of the above solutions. Break the task down into manageable pieces, then give yourself one tiny task to get your momentum going. Indulging in a nice reward for doing the dreaded task also works well.

✎ Make a list of everyday tasks you have been procrastinating on (we'll take on more difficult tasks in the next section). For each task, decide how you want to begin it and carry it out. Do you want to give yourself one tiny task to get your momentum going? Do you want to break it down into manageable pieces? Or do you want to indulge in a reward after completing it? Write your solutions.

Once each task is complete, ask yourself how well the solution worked. Over time you may find that one solution works better for you than another.

Beat procrastination

Occasionally procrastination can be very hard to overcome. Here's a way you can beat it and accomplish those tough tasks.

- Make a list of the difficult items you need to do that you have been putting off.

- For each item write down your excuse(s) for not having completed the task already. Maybe there is a money problem, or you do not think you have enough education or the proper qualifications. Whatever it is, just write it down and don't worry about how to solve it right now.

- After each item's excuse(s), write down the benefits you currently enjoy because you are procrastinating on these tasks. Yes, you are receiving a benefit for not doing the task; otherwise you would have done it by now. For example, if you wrote down that you do not have enough education, then the benefit you are receiving right now by not getting an education is that you have more money than you would if you were spending it on school. Another benefit of this same item is that you have more time to do what you want instead of spending it in school.

- Finally, look at all the reasons you have listed as excuses for procrastinating, and the benefits you are receiving. Do these still make sense? In other words, are the excuses you make for not doing a task underscored by benefits? Are these benefits really that important? Are they important enough to stick to your excuses?

Here's what one item on your list might look like:

Tasks	Compare excuses with benefits	
Item	Excuse	Benefit
Learn Spanish	Do not have enough education	Have more money than I would if I were spending it on school More time to do what I want instead of spending it in school

Table 7: Compare excuses with benefits

✎ Look over your list. With the excuses and benefits in mind, determine which of the tasks you truly want to—or need to—accomplish. Highlight those tasks.

Use what you learned in Part One and Part Two of this book to set goals to achieve the task. Then use the tiny task/break it down/ reward method you learned in this chapter to beat procrastination and begin.

Procrastination is not a harmless little habit. Careers fail, marriages fail and businesses fail because of it. Change your "do-it-later" habit into a "do-it-now" habit. Now.

Chapter Twenty-six

The Power of Motivation

Your vision statement and "Whys"—the benefits of achieving your goals—are there to motivate you whenever enthusiasm for your tasks dwindles.

Whether you succeed in reaching your dreams depends largely on your ability to persevere. The fact is, most people quit three feet from the finish line.

"Why would anyone do that?" you ask. Because no one knows when the finish line will come until they finally cross it.

Motivation is a powerful factor. Motivation is what will drive you over the finish line.

You must be able to push through setbacks and obstacles until you achieve your goal. This is what successful people do—they persist, persist, and persist until they get what they want.

Some experts say the goal itself should be enough to inspire diligence toward achieving it, and there is an element of truth in that. However, the reality is that the discomforts of striving for a particular goal can sometimes cause us to lose focus.

Want to get in shape, save for a large purchase, "make the grade" in your studies? Whatever you're trying to do, the following tips will help you stay motivated and on track.

Think of the result

Can't you just see yourself pounds lighter and fitting into a nifty outfit? The key question is, how do you imagine yourself *feeling*? Healthier?

Sexier? More self-confident? When you develop the ability to picture your goals and imagine what the results will be, you are more likely to stay motivated.

Many people have found it helpful to compose a "dream board" which is an arrangement of images that represent the goal. For instance, if you were saving money for a tropical beach vacation, then you'd get some travel brochures or create a collage of pictures from a magazine of blue ocean, palm trees, exotic fruit drinks . . . you get the idea!

🖉 Think of a goal for which you losing motivation. Give detailed thought to what the end result will be. Picture yourself having achieved your goal. Use all five senses. For another goal, compose a dream board. Which of these best stirs you to action?

Reward yourself for small victories

It's human nature to want results now. However, some worthwhile goals may require much effort and time to accomplish. Don't let that deter you. You've learned to set small goals that will eventually add up to big results. Keep yourself motivated by setting up a self-reward program for achieving each of those small goals.

If pushing through a tedious project causes you to dawdle or get easily distracted, you might find that giving yourself small rewards as you complete small chunks of work will keep you motivated.

Perhaps you will only get a cup of coffee when you've finished filing half of the pile. Or maybe you'll take a stretch or call a friend (briefly) when you've dealt with twenty e-mails. Keep the rewards small but frequent enough to maintain your momentum. Doing so will keep you energized and motivated.

Draw inspiration from others

Sources of inspiration to stay motivated can come from success quotes, lyrics, movies that depict people who reached their dreams through hard work, or even speaking with others who have achieved what you're working toward.

Tape success quotes to your computer. Buy that CD with those great lyrics and listen to it, or buy the DVD and watch it when you need a burst of motivation. Speak with successful people, mentors and life coaches, and let them inspire you.

If your focus begins to fade or you skid on a patch of discouragement, you may find it helpful to identify an accountability partner who will encourage you to stay the course. And, in instances where your partner is also striving toward an accomplishment, you'll experience the magic of motivating each other toward success.

✎　　Make a list of CDs and DVDs that motivate you. Buy them. Place dozens of success quotes all around you. Find someone to encourage you.

Use success creeds, questions and stimulants

A *success creed* is used to define a particular value which you intend to adhere to during the pursuit of your success.

The following are sample success creeds:

- I will give 100 percent effort and thought to all that I say and to all that I do.
- I will treat others in such manner that I will never be ashamed to face the person I greet in the mirror each morning.
- Everything I do and think will be the right choice for my family.
- I will direct myself toward prosperity and success by keeping my energy and thoughts focused on the goals I've set for myself.

Use as many different success creeds as you like. Use business-related success creeds and family-related success creeds.

✎　　Write one or more success creeds to focus your values and motivate you to do your best. Place them where you can see them.

A *success question* is used to control the focus of your internal thoughts. As your mind is constantly in thought, various external influences throughout the day control what your internal thoughts are focusing on.

Regularly reviewing success questions intrigues your internal thoughts, prompting your mind to focus on the topic of your question, while lessening external influences.

Here a few sample success questions:

- "What can I do for exercise today?"
- "What can I do today that will assist in my mission to gain and keep an average body weight of ____lbs?"
- "What can I do today to help in achieving my goal to achieve two million in sales this year?"

✐   Write one or more success questions to intrigue and focus your internal thoughts. Place them where you can see them throughout the day.

Similar to the success quotes and lyrics mentioned above, a *success stimulant* is simply any quote or phrase that comes to you which you find motivating or stimulating.

The following are examples of success stimulants:

- As one door closes, another bigger and better door opens.
- You cannot get something for nothing, but you can have the best of everything when you give full measure for the good you wish to receive.
- I am now in charge of my life through the seemingly magical habit of goal setting. I am now open, receptive, and obedient to its rich assistance and guidance.

✐   Write one or more success stimulants that motivate you to press on. Place them where you can see them . (Right about now would be a good time to purchase a bulletin board.)

✐   Print your success creeds, success questions and success stimulants on a business card format and carry a set of them with you, in your wallet, for instance. In a lost moment pull out the cards and thumb through them to remind you of your mission and goals so they will motivate you.

Visualizing the end result, celebrating small victories along the way, and drawing inspiration and encouragement from others and from yourself are four powerful, easy-to-implement methods of staying motivated toward reaching your goals. Whenever a new song, movie or quote motivates you, add it to your collection!

Bonus Ideas

How to recharge yourself

Whenever you feel tired, discouraged, or lacking energy, stop whatever you are doing, and take five deep breaths, inhaling and breathing out very slowly.

Repeat the following affirmations:

I am strong and healthy. I am in full control. I can accomplish anything I wish.

I am now charged with energy and vitality to do the task before me.

Exercise

Exercising three or four times a week can help you reduce stress and produce a sense of balance, discipline, order and control in your life. Maintaining physical health is also a great way to stay motivated.

Chapter Twenty-seven

Communication

You need to be a good communicator to make the best use of your available time and the available time of others. You must be able to let people know where you stand and where you are heading. You also need to listen to and understand other people's needs.

Most communication is based on assumptions, opinions, ideas, theories, guesses, and personal experiences. It can be a challenge for two people with different assumptions, opinions, ideas, theories, guesses, and personal experiences to grasp each other's meaning. *Understanding* is grasping the meaning of what is said. If we do not understand, the time spent communicating is wasted.

Communication also includes keeping an open mind. Keeping an open mind means you are willing to listen and hear what others have to say. Doing so frequently saves time.

So how do you know if you communicate a message effectively? You could wait and see if the result you hoped to achieve by communicating is met. Or you could encourage others to ask questions and provide feedback.

The feedback sandwich

Feedback is an important technique you can use to check if your communication efforts are up to par. As mentioned above, you can gain feedback from others. You can also give it.

Because giving and receiving negative feedback can be difficult, a beneficial—and efficient—means of doing so is the "feedback sandwich."

A feedback sandwich consists of criticism "sandwiched" between praise. This allows both you and the receiver to look at the negatives in light of the positives, and puts criticizing in a constructive context.

In short, it means you tell somebody something you appreciate, then some room for improvement, and finally some more of what you appreciate.

So you provide feedback on behavior you want somebody to keep and behavior you want somebody to change.

Here are some tips on how to make a better feedback sandwich:

- Feedback (positive or negative) should be directed toward a person's performance. It should not be personal or directed toward their character.
- Praise should not flatter the ego; it should reinforce and encourage desired behavior. The recipient should walk away more educated about what worked, not just "feeling good."
- Be specific in both praise and criticism. "I really liked when you did XYZ . . ." "When you said so-and-so, I noticed that . . ." "I thought your use of such-and-such was . . ."
- Criticism especially should be *constructive, well timed,* and *targeted.*
- *Constructive* criticism is clear, objective, and employs "I" statements rather than "You" statements. It offers realistic alternatives or suggestions for improvement.
- *Well-timed* criticism is sensitive to the time, place, and situation. It is offered soon enough after the performance to be relevant, but not so soon after as to touch on something that this still raw. It is given privately or publicly, depending on whichever is more appropriate, and is often preceded by a heads-up that feedback is coming.
- *Targeted* criticism hones in on specific skills or practices that are within the person's control. It avoids using extreme phrases like "always" and "never."
- Use nonverbal communication to package the sandwich. Let your eyes and body language express your feelings. Dramatic pauses can go a long way. A softening of the voice can make that room-for-improvement easier to digest.
- Allow the recipient to respond—feedback does not need to be a one-way street. If recipients feel the need to defend themselves or explain their actions, allow them to.

Know when you need not (and maybe even should not) use the sandwich. There are situations where using the sandwich will feel (and be) inauthentic, contrived, or insulting[i].

The power of thoughts and words

There is much evidence to support the idea that our thoughts and words are very powerful and go to make up our world reality.

"With our thoughts we make our world." - Gautama the Buddha

"Energy follows thought." - Annie Besant - *Thought Power: Its Control and Culture*

"We become what we behold." - William Blake

"Man creates his own disharmony."- Hazrat Inayat Khan

With the above in mind, let's take a closer look at some of the words and phrases we use and their deeper meaning as they relate to efficient communication:

- "Yes but" is a phrase we use to negate an opinion or idea that was expressed. Listen to yourself when you speak. Is "yes but" a common part of your speech? "Yes but" is a communication blocker. A good option for acknowledging what the other person says and following it with your own opinion is to use "yes and." "Yes and" improves the energy of the communication in two important ways. First, it acknowledges and validates the other person's point of view. Second, it keeps the flow of the conversation in place. Both reduce the chance for time-consuming disagreements.

- Words can be empowering or disempowering. For instance, "got to," "have to," and "must" usually denote a feeling of no choice. Again, listen to your self-talk and the speech of others to get a sense of what's going on at an inner level.

- "Should" is a good one to be aware of, as there is usually a feeling of guilt behind it. Do you ever find yourself saying, "I should go and do XYZ"? Used this way, "should" means "if I don't I will feel bad."

- We also have "never," "forever," and "always." These are gross generalizations and are rarely true. For example, "She always gets that look on her face when I come home late" and "You never buy me anything nice anymore." These statements reflect the perception of the person speaking, not the reality of the matter. Such statements do not provide clear, effective communication; instead they hinder it,

93

as the speaker's true thoughts, needs, and concerns are not verbalized.

- "Try" is another interesting little word. You may have seen a demonstration of this when someone is asked to "try" to pick up a pen. You do not "try" to do something. You either do it, or you do not. Another example: You ask someone to do something for you. They reply that they will "try" to do whatever it is you have asked. You can be pretty sure with that sort of reply your request will not be honored.

🖉   Consciously listen to your speech patterns for a day to determine which of the conversation-inhibiting words and phrases you use. Or ask a close friend or relative to listen and let them repeat the words and phrases back to you.

Write the conversation-inhibiting words and phrases you want to replace. Next to them, write the word or phrase you want to use instead. Finally, practice inserting them into conversations until you use them naturally whenever you communicate.

You may be surprised and delighted at what a difference changing your words can have on your communication with others, and in other areas of your life.

Chapter Twenty-eight

Delegate

To delegate is to assign power and responsibility to another person to carry out specific activities. Delegating is yet another effective way to save you time.

People use many excuses for not delegating. Their reasons are usually unfounded.

- "I could do it perfect myself."
- "I don't know if I can trust him to do it."
- "He isn't qualified to do it."
- "He doesn't want any extra responsibilities."
- "I don't have the time to show anyone how to do it."
- "There is no one else to delegate to."
- "He already has enough to do."
- "I don't want to give up this task because I like doing it."
- "I'm the only person who knows how to do this."
- "She messed up last time, so I'm not giving her anything else to do."

Assume that most people want added responsibilities (don't you?). Assume they are keen to learn. Recognize that any short-term training investment on your part will pay off for you (and for others) in the long-term. Look around. Even if you're not the boss, there are people who will help you if you approach them in the right way.

Delegation is typically found in a business environment. However, it is also practical in a home environment. Most of the above excuses apply within families when it comes to sharing the family workload.

What to delegate

Don't delegate what you can remove. If you shouldn't be doing an activity, then perhaps you shouldn't be giving the activity away to others. Eliminate it.

Following are several routine home and business activities. Delegate as many as possible, even if you don't want to:
- Fact-finding assignments
- Preparation of rough drafts of reports
- Problem analysis and recommended actions
- Collection of data for reports
- Photocopying, printing, collating
- Data entry
- Cleaning the house
- Doing the laundry
- Taking care of your toddlers

At work, delegate tasks that are not part of the core expectations that have been placed on you.

For small businesses, tasks you may be able to delegate may include accounting, Web site design, deliveries, hardware upkeep, software help, graphic design, travel arrangements, patenting, legal issues, and even HR functions such as payroll. There are certain tasks you should not, or perhaps cannot, delegate, such as performance reviews, discipline, and firing.

When you delegate, don't give out assignments haphazardly. As stated above, invest short-term time in training to gain a long-term increase in productivity. Others may end up doing a better job than you or finding new ways to complete a task.

Delegation is not abdication. Someone else can do the task, but you're still responsible for the completion of it, and for managing the delegation process.

At home, delegate when appropriate, as you need to.

How to delegate

Now you know you need to delegate, and you have ideas of what you should delegate. So how exactly do you delegate?
Here's how:
- Delegate to the right person. Don't always give tasks to the strongest, most experienced or first available person.

- Keeping the above in mind, spread delegation around and give people new experiences as part of their training.
- Communicate in such a way that the task, standards and outcome are clear: what needs to be done, when it should be finished, and to what degree of quality or detail.
- Delegate the objective, not the procedure. Outline the wanted results, not the method.
- Be sure to delegate the authority with the responsibility. Don't make people come back to you for minor approvals.
- Trust people to do well and don't look over their shoulder or check up on them along the way, unless they ask.
- Ask people to provide progress reports. Set interim deadlines to see how things are going.
- Get feedback from employees to ensure they feel they're being treated properly. A simple "How's it going with that new project?" might be all that's needed.
- Be prepared to trade short-term errors for long-term results.
- When you finish instructing, the last thing to ask is, "What else do you need to get started?" They'll tell you.
- Once the delegated task is complete, give praise and advice (feedback sandwiches), and additional responsibilities.

✎ Make a list of tasks you can delegate. Beside each task, specify the following:

Task/wanted results	Who	Realistic to ask?	Time frame
Clean the bathroom every Wednesday	My daughter	Yes. I only have to let her know where I leave my cleaning stuff.	Weekly
Bring the garbage outside every Thursday	My son	Yes. He is old enough and strong enough.	Weekly

Visit my mother every Sunday	My two sisters	The responsibility of visiting my mother every Sunday is weighing heavily on my shoulders. I could ask my sisters to share this load.	Two out of three Sundays
Finding relevant data before I start calling prospects	Jim, our junior account manager	I am great at cold calling but finding addresses and relevant data is very time consuming and could be done by Jim.	Every Monday and Thursday

Table 8: Task delegation

✎   Next, delegate the tasks you listed, using the bulleted suggestions of the How to Delegate section that precede the table.

Your need to delegate will be ongoing. Practice delegation as a time-saving habit, one that will bring positive, rewarding results to you and to the people you delegate to.

Chapter Twenty-nine

Scheduling

Well-honed scheduling skills help you to wisely manage your time. Here's what you can do to sharpen yours.

Consider that a schedule has boundaries; it has edges. If you start to think of your schedule as a container into which you need to fit a limited number of tasks, you start to get more selective about which tasks you'll put in.

You shouldn't overschedule yourself or schedule everything down to the minute; something unexpected always comes up. Instead build time cushions in, keeping in mind that the size of cushions will vary. (I recommend that people who are in the business of crisis management, such as a financial planner, not schedule more than two or three hours' worth of work in an eight- or nine-hour day. When clients call, you have to jump.)

Schedule a quantity of personal time every day. The best way to set aside personal time is to write it into your daily appointment book.

Schedule breaks during the day. Time-management techniques are not going to give you effective solutions if you don't have the energy to give one hundred percent. Take a power nap during the day when you need to. Go to a park or play with your children for an hour if you feel overwhelmed. Take the time to clear your mind and refocus on your goals. The ideas that wouldn't come to you in the office might pour out once you are in a new environment.

Plan tomorrow today. At the end of each day, write in your journal everything you must accomplish tomorrow in the order the tasks should be done. The next day you won't have to decide what to do first, and crossing off the items you accomplish will give you great satisfaction.

On Friday afternoon, plan your schedule for the following week. By the middle of Friday afternoon, you have a good idea of what you've accomplished—or failed to accomplish—that week. This tactic allows you to mentally rehearse your schedule over the weekend so you'll have a psychological head start Monday morning. When you arrive at the office, you can hit the ground running.

Sometimes you need to accept the limitation of time. During some periods in our lives, there is clearly not enough time to do everything we would like to do, for instance, if you are a parent of small children, or if you are trying to combine home management with holding an outside job. In these cases, we must recognize we have limited time and learn to omit less important activities to free up time for those which are essential.

At other moments you simply have to minimize working hours. It may be necessary to simplify your tasks. The family can plan simpler meals, adjust standards and take over simple tasks to help put more time into your schedule.

You need to balance the use of your time. Yes, prioritize reaching your goals, but also divide your time to develop and keep happy family relationships and friendships, to rest and sleep. You need to enjoy activities such as playing tennis, golf or swimming. Sometimes and you need quiet time for yourself to clarify your own values and feelings, to start or develop a hobby or work interest, even to preserve your sanity! Good goal-setting and time-management techniques will give you room to schedule the time.

Chapter Thirty

Organize Your Work Space

To use your time well you MUST have an organized work space. Every moment looking for a pen, a file, or a misplaced check not only means wasted time but it can add to your stress level and interfere with your ability to focus on your work. Clutter breeds confusion. Clutter causes you to be so focused on what you're searching for that your main purpose suffers. Don't get stuck in that activity trap.

"Won't organizing take time?" you ask.

It doesn't have to take much time at all. After carefully studying clutter, I estimated it takes around ten to fifteen minutes to clean up a desk, while it can take as much as thirty minutes to find lost paperwork. In other words, organizing is well worth the time.

Storage

Give yourself at least fifty percent more storage space than you currently need. Before you can declutter, you'll need places for items—and for future items—to go. Invest in an affordable filing cabinet or filing bins, and an inexpensive shelving unit to give yourself more surface space. Place them where they will be easily accessible but not in your way.

Declutter

Begin with the stuff lying around that you don't need. Throw it in the trash. It's taking up space and may be confusing you about what's important. Do the same with junk mail.

Take out the trash.

File papers you already have designated, labeled folders for.

Recycle unwanted magazines. Organize the ones you want to keep. Magazine files are an easy-to-access means of storage and fit neatly on a shelf.

Give everything a home. This includes your cell phone and keys. If you leave your personal and work belonging floating around you'll waste time trying to find them.

Place phone lists, calendars and other daily needed items on your newly cleaned desk within easy reach.

Once a week toss out the junk, clean up, and file your documents.

Organize your files

Invest a few minutes organizing your file cabinet. You may prefer to alphabetize your folders, or to order them from most used to least.

Create any new files you need.

Be sure all folders are accurately labeled so you can easily locate them when needed. Apply the KISS rule (Keep it Simple Stupid). By keeping labels simple, you will not feel stupid later.

Do the same with your computer files.

Consider placing files of paid bills and other important papers—such as birth records, your marriage license, passports, proofs of insurance, medical records, financial statements, and warranties—in their own cabinet. Again, be sure to label the files specifically so there are no confusions later.

Ideas and issues that relate to a certain project can rob you of your ability to think straight and accomplish other projects. Put them together in a file so you can keep your mind free to keep going.

Filing hints

Here are some super tactics for organized filing:
- Get colorful. Buy folders of different colors, each color representing a specific category. For example: green folder is for bank accounts, blue folder is for health records, red folder is for utility receipts, and so on.
- Use tickler files for papers you access often, and keep them within reach. Tickler files free up desk space and allow for quick retrieval of those documents. With a 45-file tickler system, the present month is organized by using 31 tickler files, plus there are 12 monthly files, 1 general file for this year, and 1 file for next year. The expense? One 45-pocket file and 45 individual folders.

- Create a unique folder for each day of the month, one for the 1st day of the month, 2nd day, 3rd day, and so on. This only takes a few minutes, and once you're done, you have an efficient system for organizing papers and scheduling your tasks. Place these newly labeled folders into the 45-pocket file.
- Here's how this filing system works. Let's say your credit card bill arrives on June 4th, but it isn't due until the 20th. You may put it in the Day 15 folder, or Day 10 to give you some leeway. Do the same for other notes or papers that have a deadline. By using this method, it would be hard for you to miss out on any important date or occasion.
- In the general yearly file, you can place items that are not time specific which you do not want to lose. If the items apply to next year, place them in that file.
- Each morning empty that day's file pocket on your desk and decide on how to carry out the necessary tasks.

Organize your home work space

Your home is also a work space where activities run smoothest—and you waste as little time as possible—when it is well organized. Many of the above suggestions apply to organizing your home space as well. Here are few additional tips tailored to various areas of your home:

- In the kitchen, keep your table and countertops clear. A clean and organized working surface will enable you to be more time efficient. Also organize your kitchen drawers. A pencil shouldn't be with the knives, spoons and other utensils. Spare smoke detector batteries shouldn't be buried under pizza delivery ads.

- Keep a box or small storage bin handy that will serve as your multi-purpose box whenever you pick lost objects in your house. You can use this box after cleaning a room or making an inventory inside your closet. Make sure that the owners of those objects return them to their proper places.

- Go through your belongings and just keep the things you need or know you will use again. Give to your relatives or to charity your old clothes that are now too small for you. This applies to your other belongings as well. Upon checking an item, just ask yourself, "Will I still find use for this thing in the future?" If the answer is no, then give it away or dispose of it. Then properly organize whatever is left.

- Do not buy bulky appliances or office equipment. Your house or office should have enough space for movement and accessibility for items you need for your daily tasks.

If you want to learn more about organizing your home and life, I recommend *Eliminate Chaos: The 10-Step Process to Organize Your Home & Life* by Laura Leist. *Eliminate Chaos* is a user-friendly system for organizing each room of the house, including the kitchen and pantry, closet, garage, home office, and children's rooms. If you are primarily interested in organizing your work space I recommend *Organizing Your Work Space, Revised Edition: A Guide to Personal Productivity* by Odette Pollar. This book discusses how paper backlogs develop and how to avoid them, how to manage your desk and papers, and keeping clutter away.

Chapter Thirty-one

Streamline Your Tasks

Always look for ways to streamline your tasks, both on the job and at home. You will accomplish more in less time, so you will reach your goals faster and have more and better quality time for family, recreation and leisure.

Following are a few suggestions to get you started.

Streamline tasks on the job

Here's how to streamline time when dealing with the ongoing paper mountain on your desk.

- Throw it away. You should throw a paper away as soon as you pick it up and notice you can do without it.
- Could you delegate it to someone? Give it away.
- Next, make three piles of papers.
  - In the closest pile are items that should be acted upon.
  - In the next pile are items to be filed. Save them till the end of the day instead of filing them one at a time. It's a great time saver. (Save even more time—delegate the filing once a day.)
  - In the last pile are papers to be read. If you don't want to read a whole magazine, just copy or tear out the relevant pages. Recycle the rest of it.

If most of your tasks are handled on a computer, then take a few minutes to backup your data regularly and store it in a safe place. It can take days to recover what you have not backed up.

If you have a work mailbox or e-mail, do not give your addresses to anyone who isn't immediate family or associated with your business. This will save you time, and keep you organized.

Reduce interruptions during your best working hours. You can carry out twice as much in one quiet hour as in two regular hours of frequent interruptions.

Make the temperature just right. Temperature is a factor that could either irritate or motivate a person to work. Temperature should be just right and the senses should be tempered with pleasant stimuli during work. Not having to stop work to pull on a sweater or to cool off with trips to the water cooler allows you to focus on your tasks.

Streamline tasks at home

The more you streamline necessary tasks at home, the more time you will have for family activities. The following suggestions are easy to do and effective.

As at work, we also have paper piles at home. When you receive bills or other important papers in the mailbox, be sure to deal with them swiftly. If you receive junk mail, toss it. Junk mail has nothing to offer us. Do the same with e-mails.

Never put garbage anywhere. More so, don't let these unnecessary objects hide inside your car, cabinets, closets, or under your bed until they become little monsters of their own.

Clean as you go. Always follow the "on the fly" philosophy: close an open drawer when you pass by it, empty a full wastebasket, pick up a clothing item lying on the floor and hang it up. This is a simple way to streamline your tasks as well as maintain a habit of cleanliness. You may involve other people in this habit too.

Chapter Thirty-two

Snuff Out Time Robbers

You've tried this before—creating a to-do list, scheduling appointments and booking projects. You have started the day on the right foot, determined to get on top of things. But as you carry on through the day you see the time and are shocked that you only carried out half of what you planned.

Why does this happen?

The answer: time robbers. Activities, events, and people can all rob you of your time.

Following are the worst time robbers, and solutions for putting an end to them.

E-mails

E-mails have helped save a lot of time and money for many people. Instead of the old-fashioned snail mail, more individuals rely on e-mail to get their messages across faster, cheaper, and more conveniently.

However, there is a downside to using e-mail as a means of communication. Many people check their e-mails frequently throughout the day, thereby hampering their productivity. Some have become addicted to e-mails and spend hours reading and replying.

Below are tips to make e-mails work for you.

- Check your e-mails twice a day, maximum. Suitable times would be first thing in the morning (to take care of urgent matters) and at the end of your work day (to catch up with last-minute concerns).

- Write and reply briefly. Be clear and to the point. Don't overcomplicate an explanation.
- Pick up the phone. Several minutes spent in replying to e-mails can be shortened tremendously by just calling the person. You'll get faster responses and you'll end up saving a lot of time. And of course, the personal touch is priceless.
- Terminate spam. Spam messages are very prevalent nowadays. Not only can they waste a lot of your time, but they can be very annoying as well. To prevent spam, don't spread your e-mail address around. If you can, make your e-mail address more intricate. For example, use marschall_jones27543@yahoo.com instead of marschall_jones@yahoo.com. If you're inserting your e-mail address into Web sites and messages, you may replace @ with "AT." For instance, write down marschall_jonesATyahoo.com instead of marschall_jones@yahoo.com.
- Get your e-mail across. Sometimes your e-mail could mistakenly be regarded as spam, and this would waste your time in composing that message. To prevent such occurrence, be careful with your choice of words. Avoid words or phrases that trigger the spam filters. Some words to avoid: free, money, sex, amazing, limited offer, naked, opportunity, debt, loans, lottery, retire, urgent.

Internet

Studies show that many of today's workers spend a lot of their time surfing the Internet. If you are one of these people, you are wasting time and costing your employer money. Many businesses are cracking down, and many Internet surfers are being shown the door.

Phone calls

You don't have to answer every time it rings.
To avoid wasting time with phone calls try the following:
- If you have blocked a certain time for working on a task do not let phone calls interrupt your momentum. Turn off your phone for two hours while you complete your task. If that is too much, then do it for one hour or for thirty minutes. While you may feel that you need always be "on call," the truth is that you are losing productivity by allowing continual interruptions to your workflow.

- If you have a receptionist or an assistant, ask that your calls be held for the allotted time (making exceptions for those who need it—like your boss).
- If you must answer a phone call and the person can wait, ask them for a time when you can call back and discuss the issue. Not only will you set boundaries with your time but you can be prepared to deal with the call without other distractions.

Telephones require the use of your hand, which makes it difficult to do other tasks when you are talking. Invest in a headset if you can. It will free up both of your hands so you can do other things while you talk.

Drop-in visitors

"Do you have a minute?" will always take longer.

If you cannot finish a task without a coworker stopping in to ask you for a minute of your time, you may find your whole day is occupied with "one minute" issues. Often the individual will get comfortable and discuss many more things than they initially came to you with.

While some positions do require an open-door policy, or you may not have an office you can close the door to, it is important to have uninterrupted time in your day to complete the tasks on your list.

To avoid wasting time with drop-ins try the following:

- Change the layout of your desk so you're not facing traffic. Otherwise you encourage interruptions.
- If you store materials or files that people have to access frequently, move them to another area.
- Block off your time for priorities. Handle larger, important projects early in the morning, before you read your e-mail and before interruptions are likely to occur. Schedule a quiet hour to create essential private time.
- Tell coworkers or subordinates that you like work on your own until 9:30 a.m. Only then do you accept meetings.
- Schedule the time you are not available and stand by your decision.
- Isolate yourself. Close your door. Put up a do-not-disturb sign. Work in a conference room. If you work in an office, take a day to telecommute from home if necessary.
- Don't feel obliged to have an open-door policy. This allows people to manage your time on their terms, not on yours. Open door means you're *generally* available for honest

communication from any level. It doesn't mean you're *always* available.

- If you have an assistant, set up clear guidelines about what kinds of interruptions are fitting, so he or she can screen visitors. The assistant should have the authority to schedule a meeting, or divert an inquiry to someone else.
- If you must deal with a situation or individual, ask for the details and suggest you find a time to sit down and discuss it. Schedule it so they know you view it as important and want to give them your time.

When someone walks in without an appointment you still have several options to minimize the interruptions:

- When someone asks for a few minutes of your time, respond with "Sure, how about if I come by your office at 2 o'clock this afternoon?" This gives you more grip on your agenda.
- If they insist it's urgent, ask them how many minutes they need, then agree to that time (or tell them how much time you can give them).
- Ask subordinates to "save up" items of importance and deal with them in a bunch at an appointed time.
- Stop people from telling stories. Interrupt them and say, "Can you summarize how I can help you in one sentence?" If they ramble on, say, "Okay, so how can you sum up what you need from me?"

Prevent people from staying too long:

- When someone walks into your office or cubicle, immediately stand up. That way, your visitor is less likely to sit down and get comfortable.
- If you must, place a binder or a briefcase on visitors' chairs, to discourage people from sitting down if they happen to drop in (or remove chairs altogether).

The next suggestions may sound a little rude and should only be considered for individuals who just won't take a hint:

- Invent a meeting that you have to go to. Confess that you promised to call someone back about a confidential matter at exactly this time. Go make some photocopies. This will bring a meandering discussion to an end.

- Set a time limit. Then check the time in an obvious way, and make sure to announce the end of the allotted time when it occurs.

Be careful that your tactics are not counterproductive to the organization. What may benefit you as an individual may be harmful to the team. Isolating yourself might frustrate others, or cause them to waste their own time because you weren't available for help.

Meetings

People in meetings all day are not getting jobs done!

Meetings have their place. They are an important way to deal with group issues, create plans and get feedback. What is a problem is when meetings are called on the spur of the moment with little preparation and no plan. When these meetings start each person has a separate agenda. If the purpose of the meeting is unclear and the participants unprepared are you going to come to a clear decision?

To avoid wasting time, try the following the next time you schedule a meeting:

1. Schedule meetings for the end of the day or week so all involved can arrange their workflow and jump right into their tasks the next morning.
2. Create an agenda giving each item a time allotment. Prioritize the agenda so the most important issues are dealt with first.
3. Send the agenda to each participant a day or more in advance so they can come prepared.
4. Try to get the members seated in time. If one or two members are going to be late and everyone else has to wait for them, that will upset the pace of the meeting.
5. Cell phones, of course, must be switched of and external calls on land phones must be deferred.
6. Focus on getting a solution—scheduling another meeting should not be the solution although it may be a part of completing the plan.
7. A person should give a summary at the end of the meeting, so that the members leave with clear knowledge of what was accomplished and that it was not just a meaningless discussion.
8. If the issue can be dealt with on the phone or through e-mail don't plan a meeting.

Inability to say no

The general rule is: If people can dump their work or problems onto your shoulders, they will.

Some of the most stressed people around lack the skill to say no for fear of upsetting people. We often say yes to others because we want to please them. But when we fail to finish the task punctually, we let them down and we feel guilty. Now both parties suffer.

When asked to do something you don't have time for, keep the following in mind:

- You have a right to say no. Remember that others may take you for granted and even lose respect for you if you don't.
- Be polite but firm in saying no. You only build false hopes with wishy-washy responses. For instance, the phrase "I'll try to be there" in response to a party invitation is giving yourself an excuse to avoid a commitment. It doesn't do anyone any favors.
- Stick to your plan. If you have a written set of goals and strategies, this gives you a reason to stick to your course. "Thanks, but I already have an investment plan, so you don't need to send me a newsletter about stocks."
- When someone persists, repeat your position, perhaps in a slightly different way. "As I already said, our policy is to donate to charities that help children only."

When a superior asks you to do a new urgent task that upsets your schedule and priority list:

- Remind her that you are working on other projects that she has already identified as top priorities.
- Ask for help in deciding where the new task should fall on the list of priorities.
- Point out that you might be able to do everything, but not to the usual high standards that are expected.
- Provide suggestions or alternatives to the person who is asking. "I can't do that task today, but how about next week?" or "How about asking John instead?"

Some experts recommend keeping your answer short. This way, you can say no without feeling the need for a lengthy justification. "I'm sorry, I'm not available that night." On the other hand, others say that giving a longer answer with reasons reinforces your credibility. Let the situation decide.

When in doubt, it's easier to say no now, and then change your mind to a yes later, rather than the other way around. If you do have to say no now, here are four nice ways to do so:

1. "That sounds like a great idea! You should do that."
2. "I'd love to, but can't right now. Catch me next time."
3. "I'm so flattered that you asked me, but the timing is not good for me right now. I'd love to work on the next project with you."
4. "Have you considered asking (name) to help with that?"

Sometimes, saying yes is simply unavoidable. Here are some techniques to handle these unexpected demands:

- Tell the person you can agree to their request this time, but ask how the two of you might plan better for the next time.
- Tell them yes, but remind them they owe you one. For example, they might cover you for a shift next time you need time off.
- Tell them yes, but take control by saying you'll come back to them with a timetable. For instance, say, "I expect I'll be able to do that for you by the end of the week."
- Put a tough condition on your agreement. "If it would only take an hour, I'd be able to help, but I can't give you more than that."

Traffic

Avoid the rush hour by all means. Anticipate when traffic jams usually occur so you can adjust your commuting time. If your destination is not too far away, walking or biking are great ways to evade traffic, save money on gas, and attain or maintain a healthy lifestyle.

Extra trips

Pause every time you are going to do an activity. Always ask yourself, "What can I do along with this task to save time in the future?" For instance, let's say you are going to buy a birthday card for a friend. By asking the question, you might come up with the decision to buy more birthday cards instead of just one, to give to those who will be having their birthdays later in the year, so you don't have to go to the shop every time there is a birthday occasion.

Waiting in line

Waiting in long lines is a waste of good time. Whenever possible, avoid going to crowded places. If you cannot avoid this, pick a schedule when you expect the fewest people to show up. For example, buy your groceries on weekdays. Don't shop on weekends or paydays. You can also save time and avoid waiting in department store lines by making purchases by phone or Internet.

When you have no choice but to wait in line, don't waste your time complaining. Do something productive like reading a book, listening to educational tapes, or writing your future plans in your journal.

Television

Who can resist watching their favorite shows on TV? TV can be relaxing and entertaining, but if you really want to save time and use it to accomplish goals, turn off the TV or be strict in limiting your watching time.

✐ Read the list of distractions time robbers below. Place a check mark next to items that relate to you to show you which time robbers you need to snuff out.

Factors externally imposed	√	Factors self-generated	√
Telephone interruptions		Lack of good organization	
Meetings		Procrastination	
Social visiting		Unrealistic time estimation to do a job	
Coffee breaks		Coffee breaks	
Unexpected delays		Trying to do too much	
Mistakes of others		Lack of delegation	
Paperwork and reports		Lack of planning	
Poor communication		Lack of routine	
Employees with problems		Snap decisions that backfire	
Customer complaints		Failure to listen	
Too much routine work		Too long lunch hour	
Too many unexpected happenings		Confused responsibilities	
Spam e-mail		Making all decisions myself	
		Failure to maintain daily list of stuff that needs to be done	
		Surfing the Internet	

Table 9: Distractions and time robbers

In your journal, write the distractions and time robbers you checked, and any other time robbers that pertain to you. Beside each one, write possible solutions. The table below gives an example of challenges and possible solutions.

Challenge	Possible Solutions
Customer complaints	Put quality control on the agenda for next management meeting
Snap decisions that backfire	I will have to ask my coworkers to e-mail their questions before they can get an answer from me
Spam e-mail	Install Spam filters
Surfing the Internet	I will have to cut back on searching the Internet and browsing through irrelevant sites

Table 10 Challenges and solutions

Now the next time you are confronted with a familiar challenge you already have a solution at hand.

Chapter Thirty-three

The Ultimate Time Management Tool

Congratulations! Throughout the second half of this book, you've learned dozens of proven techniques that will enable you to make the most of your time as you work to achieve your dreams.

In this chapter you will discover the ultimate tool to consolidate those techniques into a simple, easy to use, daily time-management system.

The name of this remarkable tool?

A funnel.

We're not going to use a real funnel, but we will use the image of one. It's a great way to illustrate the optimal daily time-management process.

A funnel, as you know, is a pipe with a wide conical mouth and a narrow stem. It is used to channel liquid or fine-grained substances into containers with small openings. Without a funnel, substances would spill and be wasted.

Likewise, we work with huge quantities of goals, tasks, plans, requests, to dos and ideas each day. Because we are only physically and mentally able to handle a certain amount of work, it is important to eliminate as much as possible to lessen the amount we have to do. Using the metaphorical funnel, we can condense our workload into a manageable sum.

Here's what our metaphorical funnel looks like (following page). I'll explain how to use it shortly.

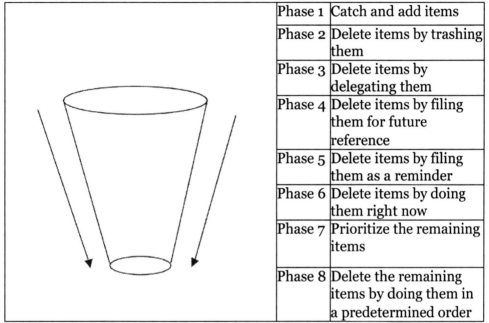

Phase 1	Catch and add items
Phase 2	Delete items by trashing them
Phase 3	Delete items by delegating them
Phase 4	Delete items by filing them for future reference
Phase 5	Delete items by filing them as a reminder
Phase 6	Delete items by doing them right now
Phase 7	Prioritize the remaining items
Phase 8	Delete the remaining items by doing them in a predetermined order

Table 11: The funnel

The funnel concept is merely an analogy. The notes you make in your journal will be your true funnel. In it you will compile all your daily goals, tasks, plans, requests, to dos and ideas, and with it you will taper those responsibilities.

Your journal

In addition to serving as a container, your journal will serve as an external brain where you keep all other items that need to be taken care of.

A common time management mistake is trying to use your memory to log the activities you need or want to do. In reality, if your head is crammed with mental notes, they will keep banging around in your mind and exhausting you. Most people need to keep track of many little details as part of their normal work. This is particularly true for workers who have to deal with several simultaneous projects and an assortment of smaller tasks.

The fact is that you simply cannot rely on your memory alone to keep track of all these details without becoming overloaded. Information overload is a growing problem and is a major source of anxiety and stress.

The good news is that most of this information overload is self-inflicted, and the remedy is simple. Dump those mental notes out of your head. Write them all down in your journal, your external brain.

The funneling process

The funneling process is easy to do if you follow a few instructions for each phase.

Here's how it works.

Phase 1: Catch and add items

The wide mouth of the funnel catches all sorts of incoming items. Some of the items dropped in are the demands of the outside world, while others are placed there by you (self-imposed), such as your short-term goals and strategies.

Again, it is your journal that is actually catching these items as you write them down.

To the "funnel" you add mental notes and other items as they come to you throughout the day.

This adding and catching is essential when you need to carry out several different tasks or different sorts of tasks, or when you have made commitments.

All those items are neatly caught in one place, as journal entries.

Here is a sample journal entry:

MONDAY, SEPTEMBER 7TH

Schedule appointment with chiropractor
Buy flowers for Mindy on way home
Do thirty-minute bike workout
Proofread John's proposal
New car brochure
Plan agenda for Friday's meeting
Invitation for business meeting at chamber of commerce
Blueprint for next year's budget plan
Call Bill on follow-up proposal
Change the coffee filter
Phone Tom to make an appointment
Brochure from Yale University
Congratulate Kevin on his birthday
Lunch with my boss

Write a report on sales
Post three pages on hubpages.com
Develop ten new ideas for marketing campaign
Bring car to the garage
Check if Randy Newman is coming to Antwerp this fall

✎   Begin filling your own journal with current and upcoming tasks, projects, home and work responsibilities, goals, strategies, meetings, appointments, and so on. Write the date of the entry at the top of each page.
     If the entry has a deadline, write its deadline beside it.

After you have finished, you will have filled one or more journal pages with tasks to be completed. Now these tasks need to be processed so that you can get them done on time.

(I have frequently been asked what to do with incoming e-mail, snail mail or recorded voice memos. I think it would be a waste of time to manually jot down all these in your journal. In this stage of your learning, it suffices to keep the inbox of your e-mail program as a separate journal. However, you should write necessary actions relating to these incoming memos in your journal, with their deadlines when applicable.)

Phase 2: Delete items by trashing them

Next, remove the junk! Reduce the tasks in the funnel by getting rid of all the items that are of no use to you now and will be of no use to you in the future.
     The primary idea of adding items to the funnel is to form a list of tasks that can and should be done. If you determine an item will be of no benefit to you, and would only impede your progress, trash it (cross it off your list).
     A quick look at our sample journal above shows two items that can be crossed off right away:

New car brochure
Invitation for business meeting at chamber of commerce

I do not want to spend time on a new car brochure, as I am not in the market for a new car right now. I'll skip the business meeting this time as it's too time consuming and has little or no payoff.
     This deleting has, within a few moments, pared down the list of tasks by two.

Phase 3: Delete items by delegating them

Earlier in this book you learned to delegate. If you have forgotten what it is or how it works, feel free to revisit that chapter.

After re-skimming our sample journal, I have found items I can delete by delegating them. I'll ask my wife to take care of these chores as she doesn't have to work today:

Schedule appointment with chiropractor
Bring car to the garage
Check if Randy Newman is coming to Antwerp this fall

In this case I will not put a reminder in my agenda because I trust my wife 100 percent. If this weren't the case, I would have added a note regarding who I delegated the tasks to and a reminder for myself to monitor whether the tasks have been taken care of.

Phase 4: Delete items by filing them for future reference

Next (notice these deletions are only taking a few brief moments to do) delete items from your journal by simply putting them away for future reference. They must be retrievable when they are needed, so you may find it handy to make a "future reference" file.

Brochure from Yale University

I don't want to throw this item away. It might contain useful information I would want to read at a later date. So I file it and cross the item off my list.

Phase 5: Delete items by filing them as a reminder

After studying the original list, I notice two items that do not need immediate attention:

Post three pages on hubpages.com
Blueprint for next year's budget plan

I write notes for each of these, file the notes as reminders under appropriate dates in my 45-folders system, and cross the items off my list.

Phase 6: Delete items by doing them right now

Now our list of items has decreased by eight. This has hardly cost any time at all. When you work on your lists you will achieve more or less the same results.

I see eleven items still open on my list. Obviously several of these items can be done with minimal effort and within a very short time frame. I can do these right now.

The benefit of working on these items now is that completing them has an immediate impact (instant gratification for accomplishing those goals) and leaves an even more concise list of remaining items.

I can easily deal with a few items by telephone:

Call Bill on follow-up proposal
Phone Tom to make an appointment

I can complete others via my PC:

Proofread John's proposal
Write a report on sales
Lunch with my boss

After I proofread the proposal and write the report, I'll send my boss a lunch invitation by e-mail, check for e-mail messages while I'm at it, and take a quick glance at the Web site hubpages.com.

On my way to the coffee machine (to change the filter) I'll stop at Kevin's desk and congratulate him personally on his birthday.

Taking care of these items will cost me a maximum of forty-five minutes, and I'll even be able to stretch my feet by getting away from my desk for a short break.

Phase 7: Prioritize the remaining items

The tasks that remain in the journal should be done one by one in a predetermined manner. Prioritizing tasks and then accomplishing each task before going on to the next will help you overcome the tendency to do too much at once.

For goals that are difficult to prioritize, there are different methods to help you do so, such as *comparing tasks* against each other and, my personal favorite, *the importance and urgency grid*. Some prioritizing methods you may come across can be so detailed that prioritizing itself would become a major time-consumer. Steer clear of such methods.

Compare tasks

✎   Write down four responsibilities you need to fulfill (you may have more, but for now we'll work with this number). Compare only two items at a time (instead of all four at once), deciding which of those two is most important. Prioritize those two.

Next, in the same way, compare the other two tasks and prioritize them. Now compare and prioritize the two most important tasks, then the two least important tasks. This will enable you find your number one priority, your number two priority, and so on.

The importance and urgency grid

This nifty little grid is best illustrated with the figure below.

4 Quadrants Activities	Urgent	Not Urgent
Important	1	2
Not Important	3	4

Table 12: Importance and urgency quadrants

Quadrant 1: Urgent and Important

If someone wants a task completed by 4 p.m. (and the task is also important to you), and it's now 3:50, and you haven't finished the work yet, it's obviously urgent and important.

Crises

A crisis is an urgent and important situation that must be dealt with. What is the best time-management approach when a crisis falls in your lap?
1. Don't overreact—"shooting the messenger" is counterproductive in the long run. If people are afraid to communicate problems or emergencies because of your overreaction to their news, they may wait as long as possible or even stop telling you when things go wrong. You need to accept that mistakes will happen.
2. Figure out if it's a real crisis or if it just seems like one. Often you'll discover that what appears to be an urgent crisis turns out to be nothing at all. A real crisis is something that is important that needs your immediate attention. If the situation is a real crisis, then you may have to drop everything you are doing and deal with it. If it is not a real crisis, and it doesn't need your immediate attention, you can often delegate it and treat it as a training experience.
3. Avoid "management by crisis"—Management by crisis is allowing unexpected events, problems or emergencies to dictate your

priorities and actions. Sometimes we do need to react quickly to a crisis and contain it before it does more damage. The problem comes when crisis management becomes the routine rather than the exception. If you spend more of your time putting out fires than doing your work, you are managing by crisis.

When crisis management becomes the routine, it can easily lead to what Stephen Covey[ii] refers to as "urgency addiction." People who are addicted to urgency enjoy putting out fires, they like stepping in and solving problems, and their bosses often reward them for doing so. They have no incentive to avoid or prevent the fires because they get a payoff every time they put one out.

When crisis management becomes your normal way of doing business, it's usually pointing to a more fundamental problem that you need to solve.

An old Chinese proverb says, "The superior doctor prevents sickness. The mediocre doctor attends to impending sickness. The inferior doctor treats sickness."

Don't just treat the symptoms of the latest crisis. Cure the underlying disease and prevent it from recurring.

Quadrant 2: Not Urgent but Important

Here is where you should try to spend most of your time. This is the quadrant where you work to accomplish long-term goals.

For example, your task could be a project where you build your own information product to sell on the Internet. It doesn't matter whether you do it now or next week because it isn't urgent, but it is very important. So if you are not doing the things in this quadrant, you will not build your business.

If you're a student, Quadrant 2 also typically involves everything to do with studying. This is the box where you do most of your reading and preparing for papers and exams.

Quadrant 3: Urgent but Not Important

Typically these tasks are urgent because somebody requires something of you, but there's no advantage in it for you.

For example, your assistant pops in to say the printer broke, and she asks you to fix it because you're the only one who knows how. You're busy, and you currently don't have a single thing that needs to be printed. The task may be urgent, but it's not important to you, so it sits in box #3.

Quadrant 4: Not Urgent and Not Important

This is easy to define. It's a coffee break. Chatting on the phone. Sweeping the garage. Watching old reruns on TV.

If you want to accomplish goals, this is not the quadrant where you want to be.

Of course, it is essential for people to relax and unwind once in a while. But you should be strict in limiting your time for these activities; give them the lowest priority. If you truly want to succeed, focus on activities that will bring you fruitful results.

I use the quadrant methodology in everything I do. I constantly think, "Which box am I in right now?" If I'm in a box where I don't want to be, I quickly refocus my priorities.

Prioritizing: Helpful hints

It's good to realize that a successful prioritization routine will eliminate the need for multitasking. Concentrate on the task at hand and finish it first before skipping to another. Divided attention will result in more frequent interruptions, loss of concentration and poorer results.

Here's a great mental image. In his book *What Matters Most*, Hyrum W. Smith introduced the analogy that tasks you want to accomplish are like big rocks and small rocks. The idea is to fit your big rocks into your schedule (put them into your "bucket") first, then you fill in the rest of your available time (the gaps) with your little rocks, stuff that still must get done but is not as important.

If you fill up the bucket with little rocks first, you may not have enough room left in the bucket to fit in all the big rocks, the most important activities you want to accomplish. So fill your bucket with big rocks first. Then, even if all the little rocks don't fit, at the least the most important stuff is in there!

Phase 8: Delete the remaining items by doing them in a predetermined order

We have now funneled down (in less than an hour, according to our example) our list of tasks. The list is consolidated and in one place where they are easy to see at a glance.

With the four quadrants in mind, I can look at the remaining items in my funnel and prioritize them according to their quadrants:

Buy flowers for Mindy on way home— Not Urgent but Important (I can do that after work)

Do thirty-minute bike workout— Not Urgent but Important (I can do that after dinner)

Plan agenda for Friday's meeting—Urgent and Important (it's Thursday morning and I have to visit clients all afternoon.)

I briefly pencil in the quadrant notes in my journal. Now it's easy to determine their order and delete them from my list one by one by doing them. Albert Einstein said, "Nothing changes until something moves." What he didn't say is that in nearly every case, the thing that needs to move is you. So block some time and do those tasks.

Once you've completed all your tasks, sit back for a moment in a comfortable position and think of what you accomplished. Time management is the process of working to succeed. When we are working to succeed, we are reaching our goals. Celebrate your accomplishments!

Chapter Thirty-four

Time-Saving Devices

It would be difficult to discuss time, and managing it, without mentioning time-saving tools and equipment. These devices are designed to make you more efficient. If you're not familiar with the full range of benefits of a listed item, be sure to find out more.

- Computers, cell phones, the Internet, e-mail. These tools are common and widely used.

- Voice mail to record messages when you are gone

- Photocopiers. Of course we can make multiple prints using a printer, but a photocopier is faster and is equally as affordable.

- A memo recorder to record your ideas on a portable

- A car CD player to play educational CDs to educate you while you drive

- An autoresponder to use with your e-mail

- An iPod or Palm loaded with educational audio files and educational videos

- Conferencing tools instead of face to face meetings

- A personal information manager (PIM)—a type of application software that functions as a personal organizer

As you are able, purchase good time-saving devices that will be beneficial to you. Be sure the ones you get are not overly complicated to use. Technology should not be a hindrance in creating a better working environment. You should be able to learn the basics and receive updates on current information in the use and maintenance of sophisticated office equipment.

Chapter Thirty-five

Routines

An integral part of making your goal setting and time management a success is to implement some routines.

Make sure you keep and use a journal. In it, keep everything we've discussed.

Daily routine

First, check what tasks need to be done that day, and organize enough time for doing them. See if you have appointments or meetings scheduled that will require your time.

Next, check what tasks are required for the next few days in case you'll have to do some planning for them today. You should then consider what other tasks or major goals you might need to write, to keep propelling you toward your objectives.

Remember, you should always have enough tasks on your plate to keep you going forward, without wearing yourself out. If you don't, it will either mean not achieving your major goals, or perhaps that you've sold yourself short by setting objectives that are not dynamic enough for you.

Review your goals. These will keep your mind on what it is you are after and why. It is also a good idea to have a look back, from time to time, at the tasks you've recently completed. There is nothing more inspiring, or rewarding, than to be reminded of the progress you've already made.

When you've done your review, funnel the tasks down to size then complete all the tasks you are supposed to. Check them off when finished, and write down any new ones you've come up with.

Although it might seem surprising now, you'll relish setting more major goals and tasks. That's because success is pleasantly addicting. Once you've had a little taste of it, you'll want more because you enjoy the thrill of success.

Weekly routine

While you can't prevent the unexpected, you can lower the chances of it affecting you and your goal-setting routine. You do this through a weekly review that is one part planning and one part troubleshooting.

This weekly review should be done before you start your workweek, and include input from your family. You should begin the weekly review by going through everything you've entered into your funnel as goals—short-term and long-term—giving particular attention to the tasks you need to accomplish that week. While a daily review reminds you of the tasks need doing, if you've not planned ahead for them on a weekly basis they might surprise you, and that can be stressful. Particularly if you haven't set time aside for them.

By reviewing at the start of the week, you'll be better able to schedule and plan your tasks, which lessens your stress, ensures successful task completion, and even reduces the amount of time you'll be spending on each task.

The family is the source of most people's enjoyment, but they can also be the source of most unexpected demands on your time. The time demands are particularly stressful when you've got a lot planned. Although it won't entirely eliminate the unexpected, planning your week in advance with your family's input will lower the chances of something unexpected coming up, and lessen its effect on you.

As you schedule your tasks in advance, ask your family what demands they'll have on your time for the upcoming week, and then plan your tasks around your family responsibilities, instead of organizing your tasks first and being surprised, and unprepared, when something else comes up.

Remember, though, always ask your family as positively as possible. You don't want them ever feeling concerned about making demands on your time. And it won't be a concern to you. With proper planning you'll have more than enough time for your job, your family, and for completing all your tasks.

If you haven't yet, mark off the goals you have achieved during the week and add any new goals for the coming week. Measure your progress toward each goal so you are clear about how far you have come and how far there is left to go.

Review your "Hows." Organize your work space.

Monthly routines

Review your progress toward all of your goals as they relate to your mission and vision statements. Make sure you examine goals in all areas of your life. It is important to maintain a healthy balance between your business and personal goals.

Review your "Whys."

Review your successes. Take account of your current state of affairs.

Quarterly or half yearly

Review your mission and vision statements in relationship to your roles, values and goals, and adjust where necessary.

Don't be reluctant to go back to an earlier step and change a long-term goal or reevaluate your mission. By doing so you will continually fine-tune your direction.

Below is a routine overview form you may find helpful. Feel free to copy it or make a similar one yourself for easy reference.

Daily	Check what tasks need to be done today
	Check what appointments you have today
	Keep an eye on your goals
	Work!
Weekly	Review last week's progress
	Discuss with family or friends
	Review your goals
	Adjust if necessary
Monthly	Review your progress toward all of your goals
	Review your mission statement
	Look at your current state of affairs
	Adjust if necessary
Quarterly or Half yearly	Review your mission and vision in relationship to your roles, values and goals

Routine overview form

Evaluation

You should evaluate your efforts regularly to be sure you are on the right track.

When you evaluate, remember you are not judging the person (yourself) but merely checking if you are doing the right thing and if you are thinking the right thoughts.

You should never be afraid to change routines, goals, missions, visions or thoughts if new ones work better for you. Perhaps you meet an unexpected obstacle on your way to meeting your long-term goal. Reassess and decide if you can adapt your action plan. If you cannot adapt your plan you will need to consider why the plan went off course—did you have less power to control the situation than you thought? Were you unaware of some of the resources you would need and their cost or time obligations?

Use this new information to reconsider your goal. Is it still attainable or do you need to adjust it—either by lengthening the time or changing the outcome—and devise a new action plan?

Chapter Thirty-six

Commit to Life's Goals

To commit to your life's goals, make the following agreements with yourself:

You are serious about setting and reaching your goals.

You promise yourself that you will consistently use the skills learned to help you set and reach the wonderful success you deserve.

You agree to be honest with yourself and positive in your outlook.

You will be true to your values and design your goals around your roles.

You will set a new goal whenever one is reached.

You will not blame your upbringing, education, other people or circumstances when goal setting becomes difficult.

If necessary, you will seek out a coach or mentor to assist if you really get stuck.

You will do your best to maintain a positive and optimistic outlook, even in the face of negative events.

You are willing to gain and maintain the habit of using the simple learned skills to reach your goals of happiness and fulfillment.

You recognize that to reach your goals, you must grow personally, so you commit to consistently seek to increase your knowledge by reading, listening, and watching motivational and educational material and to taking courses which will give you a positive mental attitude and a leading edge in learning and applying that knowledge to increase your personal power and the results you get.

You will keep a list of all these activities and evaluate their usefulness regularly.

You are truly excited about the difference this will make as you direct, organize and manage your life toward success.

How to Get in Contact

Well, you have reached the end of this book, but not the end of your learning. Please share with me your successes. I'd love to hear about them. I hope you enjoyed reading this book as much as I enjoyed creating it. You are already ahead of most people because you care enough to learn more. Now all you have to do is go out and use this knowledge. I would like to see you have tremendous success!

You can reach me by using the contact information you will find at http://101lifemanagement.com

Bibliography

Books

Allen, David. *Getting Things Done*. New York: Penguin Books, 2001.

Covey, S. R., Merrill, A. R. & Merrill, R. R. (1994). "First Things First." New York: Fireside.

Covey, Stephen R. *The Seven Habits of Highly Effective People: Restoring the Character Ethic.* New York: Simon & Schuster, 1989.

Canfield, Jack and Janet Switzer. *How to Get From Where You Are to Where You Want to Be*. New York: HarperCollins Publishers, 2007.

Davenport, Liz. *Order from Chaos: A Six-Step Plan for Organizing Yourself, Your Office, and Your Life*. New York: Three Rivers Press, 2001.

Dilts, Robert. *Verander Je Overtuigingen*. Andromeda, 2006.

Dodd, Pamela and Doug Sundheim. *The 25 Best Time Management Tools & Techniques: How to Get More Done Without Driving Yourself Crazy*. Ann Arbor, MI: Peak Performance Press, Inc., 2005.

Ferriss, Timothy. *The 4-Hour Workweek: Escape 9-5, Live Anywhere, and Join the New Rich*. New York: Crown, 2007.

Grenier, Marc. *GoalPro Success Guide*. Initial Publishing, 2000.

Harris, Carol. *NLP An Introductory Guide to the Art and Science of Excellence.* Element Books, 2000.

Haynes, Marion E. *Persoonlijk Tijdmanagement*. Academic Service, 2000.

Kievit-Broeze, Ineke E. *Effectief Tijdbeheer. Handleiding voor praktisch time- en self-management*. Schoonhoven: Academic Service, 1998.

Linden, Anné and Kathrin Perutz. *Mindworks: NLP Tools for Building a Better Life*. Kansas City, MO: Andrews McMeel,1997.

Mancini, Marc. *Time Management.* Madison, WI: CWL Publishing Enterprises, Inc., 2003.

Millman, Dan. *The Life You Were Born to Live: A Guide to Finding Your Life Purpose*. H J Kramer,1993.

Pollar, Odette. *Organizing Your Work Space, Revised Edition: A Guide to Personal Productivity*. Mississauga, Ontario, Canada: Crisp Learning, 1998.

Seerup, Kevin, et al. *GoalMaker. The Complete Goal Management System, Experience the Possibilities*. Access Able Systems,1997.

Seiwert, Lothar J. *Het 1+1 van Tijd-Management*. Time/system,1988.

Smith, Hyrum W. *What Matters Most: The Power of Living Your Values*. New York: Simon & Schuster, 2001.

Turkington, Carol A. *Stress management for Busy People*. McGraw-Hill, 1998.

Web Pages

How the World's Richest 1% Get More Done by Working Less - And Less Hard, Too., http://www.simpleology.com/indexs16.php (2007-04-11)

Interactive Wheel of Life. http://www.jamuna.com/InteractiveWheel.swf (2007-04- 13)

"Law of Attraction." Wikipedia, http://en.wikipedia.org/wiki/Law_of_Attraction (2007-04-11)

Personal "Energy Audit." http://ozpk.tripod.com/0000emotion (2007-04-11)

Simpleology 101 Review. http://www.soulselfhelp.com/simpleology-101.html (2007- 04-11)

Success Discoveries. http://www.successdiscoveries.com/ (2008-09-24)

The Science of Goal Achievement. http://www.ironmagazine.com/article177.html

Walker, Karen. http://www.karenwalkercoaching.com (2007-04-11)

Wheel of Life. http://www.rainbow-journey.org/cgi-bin/multiradar.pl (2007-04-11)

Audio

Allen, David. *Ready for Anything: 52 Productivity Principles for Work and Life* (Audio CD), Simon & Schuster Audio,2003.

Bliss, Edward C. *Doing It Now (4 Pack) Cassette: How To Cure Procrastination And Achieve Your Goals In Twelve Easy Steps,* Simon & Schuster Audio, 1987.

Morgenstern, Julie. *Time Management from the Inside Out, Abridged edition,* Simon & Schuster Audio, 2000.

How to Manage Priorities and Meet Deadlines (Audio Seminars) (Audio Cassette). Nightingale Conant, 1993.

Breinigsville, PA USA
02 December 2009
228473BV00002B/7/A